Last Encore

My Time With Glenn Frey, The Eagles,
And Other Hit Artists

By

Bob "Norton" Thompson

With

Sebastian Jaymes

2nd Edition

September 2020

ISBN: 9798550072707

To
My loving and dedicated wife of 45 years
Through Thick and Thin
Toni Thompson
And
Our Daughter Summer
Who Is A Part Of It All
From Beginning To End
And
Our Grandson Carter

To Glenn Frey
My Mentor, My Friend, and My Business Partner
RIP

To The Eagles
About Whom It Has Been Said:
"They Sang Like Angels, And Partied Like Devils"
It Was a Great Ride

To Joey Dolan
We Never Saw You Fight
But We Raised Our Glasses
To You Everyday

"May the Lord keep you in the
palm of His hand
And never close his fist
too tight"

It was only Rock n Roll but I liked it

Table Of Contents

Introduction

I first met Bobby "Norton" Thompson in LA in the early seventies. We were both a couple of rock n roll roadies slinging gear and working tours for anyone that would have us. For a while, I worked for a cartage company delivering musicians instruments to the studios and live gigs all over town. Norton had a few independent cartage clients of his own that he carted around town in his van. Over the years, our friendship developed, and we'd see each other around town or at gigs. When I finally landed a plum road gig, I was able to pass some work his way. While I enjoyed the benefits of that gig with a great country-pop artist, he popped up again in Las Vegas at the Golden Nugget with headliners the Bellamy Brothers.

My boss, Mac Davis, headlined at the MGM Grand Hotel. Norton knew a few of his band, and we'd sometimes all get together after work or between shows for beers. It was always fun to wind him up and hear his stories.

No one tells a story quite like Norton. He's got the "Jersey" touch. Whereas I grew up on Cleveland's outskirts. Cleveland is a city sometimes mistaken for a boring industrial town in the Midwest…right! I had the Cleveland touch from the birthplace of rock n roll and nickel beer night riots at Cleveland Stadium. We were a perfect match. High energy and brimming with road stories and stories of the characters we grew up around in our respective Eastern cities. Cleveland characters are definitely more like Jersey or New York than Columbus, Indianapolis, or Chicago.

When Norton's years with Glenn Frey and the Eagles ended, he opened a booming rehearsal complex in the San Fernando Valley. My boss retired, and I went to work as the tour manager for the Pointer Sisters, a well-known group with a string of hits. I was back in Rock and Roll. When I was in town, we got together several times weekly to indulge our passion for golf. We added a third, a well-known musician from a big hit band, and the three of us played two or three times a week together. We'd arrive at the golf course, tee off, and begin laughing. We told war stories, laughed, and even managed to hit a couple of good shots in a row. We never stopped laughing until we were safely back home.

We even found time in our schedules for a weekend golf outing to Palm Springs, where we booked three rooms at the Ritz Carleton. We played eighteen holes immediately on arrival before we had even checked in. By Sunday night, we had finished 72 holes of golf at our musician friends club. We were the mad dogs of golf and never stopped laughing the whole time.

I moved on again and became a producer of corporate events; Norton moved to Nashville and started another successful rehearsal facility. I did well, producing worldwide events in exotic locales. I was paid in part to follow my lifelong passion for seeing the world. When I'd seen enough and slowed it all down, I moved to the California desert and wrote a three-volume memoir of my own adventures.

When Norton was ready to get his story down on paper, we got together again long distance by phone. By that time, he had been diagnosed with mild dementia, a precursor to Alzheimer's. He could misplace chunks of his memories, then find them again, but he never lost his sense of humor. I just had to dig harder to pull out the stories. I wrote in the mornings. By midafternoon, we'd talk, most days for hours, he from his home in Nashville and I in the Southern California desert. Despite his mild disability, both of us had a ball digging out the information. I'd wind him up with a story of my own, sometimes about people we knew in common. That was the trigger that got him going, and the result is this book. The stories are all Norton. I am just the humble scribe that untangled and sorted them, then whittled them into publishable form. For once, the ratio of perspiration to inspiration in my writing was about even. We hope you enjoy it.

Sebastian Jaymes

1

Call Me Norton

I was fresh off the block and relatively new to LA when a friend and I boldly weaseled our way backstage before a Dan Fogelberg concert.

"Wow, Dan Fogelberg," we thought. "Big-time!"

"Nobody's gonna believe we actually got in," I said.

We wandered around the venue for a while, then found ourselves at a loading area where a bunch of guys was unloading a truck with the band's equipment.

"Hey, put this amp onstage," someone yelled.

So, I picked up the amp and placed it where I was told and began to walk off.

The same guy shouted, "Hey, Norton!"

I turned toward him, puzzled.

"I'm Bobby Thompson," I said, "Who's Norton?"

He gave me a quick once-over. "You look just like that character Ed Norton, the sewer worker on the Jackie Gleason show. He's a funny guy."

The guy that stopped me was Tom Kelly, the guitar player in Fogelberg's band. One thing led to another that day, and they offered me my first job in rock n roll as a roadie for the band.

Tom never stopped calling me Norton, and the name stuck. I've been around the world many times over with some of the biggest bands in rock n roll, and I've made a lot of friends everywhere. If you ask anybody if they know Bobby Thompson, they might say, "Who?"

But mention "Norton" and you'll ring a bell. People always seem to remember me.

So, call me Norton.

2

Thirty Dollars And A Plane Ticket

When I was a kid, I worked for a guy named Frank. He owned a few concessions, and a waffle stand on the midway at Palisades Park in New Jersey. Palisades Park was sort of the equivalent of Atlantic City, back when both were in their heyday. Frank used to go to my dad's joint, so he knew my dad and did him a favor by hiring me. It was just me at the waffle stand until about five or six o'clock during a typical day at the park. On the weekends, there were three of us because it got very hectic.

From where our stand was located, you could see the diving horse jump off the tower. We could see all the clowns and the midway attractions. The clowns roamed around and mingled amongst the crowd. They acted as shills to rope in the customers on the midway. Acrobatic girls climbed up to high trapezes to do their act. It was like one of the rings at a three-ring circus, except it was all out in the open.

Frank also had a sit-down restaurant where customers could sit and eat and watch the performances right from their tables.

When the park closed for the season, we packed up our stuff, got on a bus, and went off to the Connecticut State Fair. At the fair, Frank had a French Fry stand and a waffle stand. The fair lasted about a week or ten days.

In Newark, New Jersey, in the summer of 1969, my friend Wally and I were doing what we could to get by. Typical street moves. Not serious money, but enough to keep the wolf away from the door.

Between the two of us, we had thirty dollars in our pockets. But we also had two one-way airline tickets to Los Angeles that were fronted to us by a travel agency friend. In 1969, Los Angeles was the place where it was all happening, and everyone wanted to be there.

Wally mentioned he had a friend in LA that would put us up and "treat us like kings," he said. He had made up his mind to go, and I went along for the ride. Who didn't want to be in LA in 1969? Swimming pools... movie stars... the Sunset Strip... free love! We left out of Newark the next day.

On the final approach to LAX, I got my first look at LA from the air. It was a big change from the part of Newark that I came from. Ocean and beaches, mountains, and an endless sea of suburbia stretched from horizon to horizon. Everything looked clean and fresh, the opposite of the dingy old east-coast sprawl I had left behind.

We stood curbside at baggage claim and soaked in the balmy breeze from the Pacific Ocean that carried a distinct LA-west-coast smell. It was a mixture of sea air and carbon monoxide—no doubt from the millions of cars that came through the arrivals area daily.

We hadn't done any advance planning apart from hooking up with Wally's pal, a barber that worked at a Hollywood shop called *Gary's*. With little knowledge of the city, we headed for the nearest exit to hitchhike our way to Hollywood.

A few rides later, we found ourselves staring through the window of Gary's Barbershop in Hollywood. Gary's place was a two-chair-shop in the heart of Hollywood at Las Palmas and Hollywood Blvd. Gary was the owner, and Wally's pal, Nick, was the number two man.

Nick was taken totally by surprise. He nearly lost it when he saw Wally. They'd only met once before at the Whiskey A-Go-Go on Wally's previous visit to LA. His jaw almost dropped to his waist. "What're you doing here?"

"Thought I'd check out the West Coast again."

Nick blurted out: "This is my friend Wally from back east."

"Who's he…" Gary said, nodding towards me.

"Bobby, Bobby Thompson, I said, how come it's so hot in here?"

"Air conditioners out."

I looked at the sad old wall unit and said, "I know a little bit about these things. I can take a look at it if you want."

"Be my guest," he said.

After I fiddled around with it for a few minutes, it began to blow out cold air. Before long, the whole shop had cooled down.

Later, I got to know Gary a little, and he took me to lunch a few times to thank me. Those lunches helped get me through some lean times.

I learned that Nick and Wally had only met once, briefly, some time back, at a club on Sunset Blvd. But he put us up anyway. Our thirty bucks weren't going to last forever. So, we hung out at the dive bar near the apartment. We hustled pool, hustled drinks, and hustled the hookers that hustled the patrons that hung-out there.

We lasted three full days at Nick's. After his live-in girlfriend had a talk with him, we were kicked out, evicted, out on the street. So, we checked in to a cheap motel nearby.

We were broke and living on what little we made at the bar. We couldn't go home to Jersey. There wasn't even anyone we could call. We still made a few bucks on the pool table at the bar, and we made a rule: we'd always save a dollar each day for a meal at McDonald's.

Eventually, our income increased from the sale of weed and other contraband that was popular on the street at the time. Then Wally and I began looking for a place of our own in Hollywood. We found accommodations at a place in Silverlake called the

Temple Of The Rainbow. The Temple was a Salvation Army for Hippies and runaways. You could always get a bed, a vegetarian meal, and a lecture on their brand of spirituality. I could walk or hitchhike from there to The Whiskey A-Go-Go each night, the happening place at that time. It was almost 9 miles.

Later we scored a house at the top of Vine Street near a monastery for $115 a month. Then Wally and I and Rachel and Terri, two girls we'd met, moved in together.

We lived in that place for three years. We did whatever we could to make a buck. We could walk to the barbershop from the house, so we still hung out there as well.

I was hitchhiking down Santa Monica Blvd near Crescent Heights in Hollywood. A car with several young girls and a guy I knew stopped near me at a light. Because I knew the guy, I began chatting him up for a ride.

Toni, the girl driving, resisted. "Uh-uh, I'm not giving you a ride… no way!" The more I worked them over for a ride, the more Toni rejected me. Then I jumped in the car anyway, and she gave in.

I noticed Toni had a cold, so I talked her into driving to the nearby Mayfair Market where we bought over the counter medications for her cold. She said she was from South Bend, Indiana, and had worked as a secretary at Notre Dame. I was immediately attracted to her and told her I was going to marry her.

I got closer to Toni and began to nurse her back from her cold.

When Bedtime came, she said she'd sleep with me if I left my jeans on. I slept in my jeans for the next six nights.

Forty years ago, Toni and I had a beautiful daughter together. And Forty-five years after I jumped in that car, Toni and I are still happily married. Over the years, life has thrown us a lot of ups and downs, and we've stuck together through thick and thin.

3

A Foot In The Door
Fogelberg, Speedwagon, Walter Egan,
The Bellamy's

Dan Fogelberg was a fine arts major in college: In his words, "No one was paying me to paint pictures, so I sang and played the piano."

He got a big break in his hometown of Peoria, Illinois when a former girlfriend called to tell him an important music agent wanted to hear him play. She took him to a frat party at a rowdy local bar to meet Irving Azoff, a University of Illinois graduate who started a local booking agency. Azoff had already landed regional band REO Speedwagon a deal with Epic Records and was on the look-out for new artists.

When Azoff took his new company to Hollywood, he sent for Fogelberg, rescuing him from near poverty in Colorado. The rest would soon become history.

I was in poverty too, when I met the guys from Fogelberg's band. It was a fluke, a chance in a million meetings. They took me in and took me on the road with them because I looked like Ed Norton, worked hard, and made them laugh. We did gigs all over the country. It didn't pay much, a few bucks, meals, and travel, but it was a lot of fun.

Tom Kelly launched a career for me when he called me "Norton." He said I looked like Art Carney; an actor that played sewer worker Ed Norton on the 1950s Jackie Gleason TV show The Honeymooners.

It wasn't long before the whole band called me Norton. Then the entire crew, sound and lighting guys picked up on it. I started wearing a hat similar to the one Norton wore on the show, and I've been Norton ever since.

The band included Tom, Denny Henson, a singer-songwriter, guitarist and pianist, drummer Ron "Crunchy" Grinnell, and Doug Livingston on Pedal Steel. They were all good guys and fun to hang out with.

Tom Kelly was also an accomplished songwriter with a string of hits. He co-wrote with a guy named Billy Steinberg. They had written hits for artists like Cyndi Lauper, Celine Dion, The Bangles, The Pretenders, Madonna, and Whitney Houston. As a band, they were the openers for Fogelberg's show and called

10

themselves Fools Gold. Like the band, Tom was an Indiana native, another Midwesterner like Fogelberg.

Grinnell's girlfriend occasionally traveled with the band. Ron would have me place a chair onstage next to the drum riser when she was there. I'd escort her to the chair before the band came out, and she'd sit right there, on stage, for the entire set. That seemed a bit quirky to me.

The most prominent character in the band was a guy they called "Balloon." He'd earned the name from a trick he was rumored to do with his uncircumcised foreskin. That was a lot more than a bit quirky. Balloon had also been known to cover his entire body in shaving cream, then go to the front desk at a hotel and ask for a razor. But as far as touring goes, I was still a mere babe in the woods back then. I hadn't even seen the road to quirky.

I toured with Fogelberg for about 3 months. When they stopped touring, I moved on.

Irving Azoff also managed the original REO Speedwagon. When Fogelberg ended for me, I went on the road with them. For a group named after a vintage 1915 light truck, they were a good band.

I worked with the original lineup of the band: Kevin Cronin on Guitar and Lead Vocals, Neal Doughty on keyboards, Bruce Hall on Bass, Gary Richrath, played Lead Guitar and Alan Gratzer was the Drummer

Early in my time with them, I was sitting in an empty audience seat after a show when Cronin, dragging his young son with him, said, "Norton, watch my kid for me," and walked away. As soon as Cronin left, the kid took off running full speed across the venue and kept going. When Cronin came back, he said, "Where's my kid? I thought I told you to watch him."

I looked him directly in the eye. "I did watch him. I watched him run from here to there and all over the place. I'm an amp-mover, not a kid watcher."

My partner Rick Kelly and me (no relation) had their stage set-up down to a science. They weren't bad guys, except for Cronin, that is, sometimes. He had this weird way of making people feel uncomfortable. He liked to pick at people's faults and continuously put them down. A favorite target was Neal Doughty, a harmless guy and a real character who always wore a hat. Cronin was all over him, rarely about his playing and mostly when he was high though it never impacted his playing. The word was when Doughty eventually got fed up with it; he quit the band. The same went for Alan Gratzer.

Bruce Hall, Gary Richrath, and Alan Gratzer were all nice guys, consistently nice. At the end of one tour, Alan Gratzer quit the band to open a sandwich shop.

We did a gig once in Canada that was on the second floor. The only way to get the gear in was up a narrow fire escape. Coming down, we broke a leg off the B-3 organ. Scrambling for help in a strange city, we finally found a repairman that was willing to come out and make the repair. He trimmed it, glued it, and put it back together. In the end, he did such a great job of repairing it we decided not to tell the band. They never knew. Don't ask, don't tell.

The REO tour had a surprise ending for Rick Kelly and me. We were breaking down the stage on what would be the last day of the tour. Tom Consolo, one of Azoff's partners at *Azoff, Baruck, and Consolo*, walked out in the middle of the load-out and bluntly announced, "Tour's over, that's it, no more tour." Rick and I were speechless. But I rebounded quickly with "Good thing we took those house-painting Jobs." Yeah, Right!

He walked away, thinking, "What the hell are those two morons talking about? House-painting... huh?"

I worked with another act in that period, a solo artist named Walter Egan. Walter was from Queens, New York, an art major turned surf-rock band member, turned solo artist for his one hit single, *Magnet and Steel*. For a time, he was produced by Lindsay Buckingham of Fleetwood Mac.

During my time with Walter, I did everything. We'd get to a town, and before I went to a load-in, I'd stop at the hotel and get a bellman. Then I'd make the rounds with him to be sure he delivered all the bags to the right rooms.

The other memorable thing about the gig with Walter was the girl singer that was always late. No matter how much you hyped the lobby call, she'd still be in her room oblivious to the time. I'd be in the lobby with Walter waiting to leave, and he'd turn to me and say, "Where is she…?"

I always thought to myself, "Where is she? You know where she is. She's up in her room with clothes scattered all over the place and an empty suitcase, that's where she is."

Then Walter would say, "Go up and get her." I dreaded it, but up I went. I'd knock on her door until she opened it. Most times, she'd be standing there buck naked with a confused look on her face and an attitude of, "What - do - you – want?"

"We need to go. The rest of the band is in the lobby, waiting for you."

Then I'd enter her room. It was always a disaster area. Clothes were literally in every corner of the room, on the bed, the floor, in the bathroom, everywhere. I'd help her gather everything up then hand it to her so she could drop it in her suitcase, no particular order, and no folding. Just jammed in one big wad. Then I'd escort her down to the lobby and into transportation. It was an everyday occurrence, every day of every road trip.

Annie was also a scrapper that could literally fight back-to-back with any man. But she could sing. Boy, could she sing.

On my way to a Walter Egan gig at a college somewhere in Jersey, my partner and I were driving down the New Jersey Turnpike. I had been going for hours by then, and he was fast asleep on the seat next to me. I slowed down for a toll booth coming up in the distance and realized I had no change to throw

14

in the basket. I yelled over to him, "Hey, wake up, I need some change. I only have bills."

Suddenly he bolted upright out of a sound sleep, stuck his hands in his pockets, then threw a handful of coins at me and leaped out the door screaming, "I quit, I quit." A rain of coins flew at me and landed everywhere. On the floor, on the dash, in my hair, and in my crotch. Meanwhile, he jumped over a barrier and a guard rail, running for the nearby woods at the bottom of the roadway's high embankment.

I scraped together enough to pay the toll, cleared the toll booth, and pulled over to the shoulder. Standing next to the guardrail, I scanned the tree line, trying to get a bead on him. I called out a few times, but he was long gone. Standing there for a few minutes, I wondered what had just happened. All I did was ask him for some coins, and he freaked out.

In metaphysics, believers say not to wake someone up too abruptly as they could be scared right out of their bodies. I shuddered… was his soulless body running through the woods like the headless horseman?

A short time later, tired out of my wits after the long drive, I got to the gig, offloaded the truck alone, and headed to the hotel for a shower. The phone rang. It was my fugitive partner. He said he was sorry and didn't know what had come over him, but he wanted to come back.

Another guy I worked with on the Walter Egan tour was Walters stage manager, Matt. Matt was a great guy with a great sense of humor. He took several vitamin pills every day and carried them in one of those little pill containers with multiple compartments. Each compartment was labeled with over the top names like, "Knock your socks off," "Blow Your Mind," "Kapow," "Wowie Zowie."

He carried no illegal drugs whatsoever, just vitamins.

Crossing the border into Canada on our way to a gig, the border cops pulled us out of line and said they had to search the vehicle. We literally had a ton or more of equipment in the back, and I protested, explaining that we were hauling musical equipment. Then I showed them the carnet bond that allowed us to transport gear in and out of the country. "We have to see these items," they said, and I responded, "What do you mean you have to see them? There they are!" I was getting frustrated. We had a show to get to, and this guy was slowing us down. Finally, I said, "If you need to inspect each case, be my guest. Just make sure each item goes back in the case the way you found it."

Then he backed off a bit. Spotting our personal luggage in the truck, he decided to inspect them instead. He pulled Matt's bag out, rummaged through it a bit, and found the pill container. "What's this?" he said, reading the captions.

"Vitamins," I replied, "he just marks them with funny labels."

Before we knew it, we were isolated and told to take two of the vitamin B tablets. The agent was having fun with us. If we got high, he would bust us and have a laugh of his own at our expense. We sat there for three or four hours while he waited for us to get high. Every so often, we'd say, "Can we go now?" "NO,"

He answered. When he was finally satisfied that we weren't hallucinating little green men or talking to God, he let us go.

We ended up being late for the show, but we hustled and got it done, and all was well, except that I cursed Matt up one side and down the other for jamming us up like that.

Jimmy Buffet was another moneymaker I worked with from the Irving Azoff stable of thoroughbred hitmakers. Buffet sold-out concerts everywhere and had sort of a cult following based pretty much on the lifestyle he sang about in his hit, Margaritaville. It was number 14 on Billboard magazine's 1977 Pop Singles year-end chart.

After a couple of tours with Buffet, I was still the new guy, a hired hand. I found the band and crew to be a big clique with no way in. No matter how hard I tried, I was still on the outside looking in. Most of them were not easy to get along with either.

Buffet had a loyal following called Parrot Heads. But I didn't get Buffet. He was always on the mic, always talking. Plus, he did too many shark songs.

I was at a Loggins and Messina show with a friend of mine. We were trying, as usual, to weasel our way backstage. Then Timmy McCarthy, the production manager with the show, saw us lurking and asked if we wanted to help out. We ended up touring with them for several weeks until Kenny Loggins had an accident and cut his hand. They took him to a hospital and bandaged him up. But that put us out of work for several weeks.

His hand ended up healing OK, but the gig didn't last too much longer after that, and the duo eventually broke up.

Another great artist I toured with for a short time was singer, songwriter, and actress Yvonne Elliman, the daughter of a Japanese mother and an Irish father. She had been in the original cast of the hit Broadway show, *Jesus Christ Superstar.* Yvonne had a couple of hit records in the 1970s and reached #1 with a song called *"If I Can't Have You." She also did an* adult contemporary cover of a Barbara Lewis hit called "Hello Stranger" that went to #1. She had a third hit that reached #5.

"Yvonne was a wonderful person, crazy in a good way, and a lovely lady." When Toni was about eight and a half months pregnant, she took us all to Hawaii, her home state, where she lived. Yvonne's parents put together a big Luau for us with a roasted pig and the whole schtick. She took us everywhere in the islands. We had a terrific time.

When I got with the band *Chicago,* I thought they were all a bunch of Holy Rollers. They were an OK bunch with a few exceptions. I heard they had a reputation as being party boys in the early days, but none of the band, except for the Drummer, drank alcohol in my time with them. There was always a bottle of wine leftover from the band's rider requirements. I'd give it to him to take back to his room. He didn't drink much more than a little wine now and then, but man, what an incredible drummer.

There was a part in the show where one of the horn players played the tambourine. When the Tambo part ended, he quickly grabbed his horn to play with the horn section. He'd throw the Tambo offstage at me like a frisbee, more like a third baseman trying to get a fast runner out at first base. Sometimes, like a first baseman, I'd have to make a long stretch. Once or twice, when I missed (The runner would have been safe), I had to run to retrieve it.

When I became a rehearsal studio owner. My co-writer, One of the Chicago band, and I played golf twice a week. We played various golf courses in Southern California. It was 18 holes of laughter. One thing from golf we can still laugh about is a particular bush on one of the golf courses we played. It was some kind of tropical foliage, big and bushy with thin leaves that grew up out of the plant then hung straight down like a Beatles haircut. You couldn't see the rest of the plant, only what looked like a giant head of hair. It reminded us of the Character *"Cousin It"* from the old Adams Family TV show. When we got to that hole, we always glanced at each other and mumbled under our breaths, "Cousin It..." Our favorite hazard was strategically placed on the right side of the fairway at about the distance the average duffer like us sliced their drive. "Cousin It" ate balls. Forget about it! If your ball landed in Cousin It, you'd never see it again. I think subconsciously, we aimed at it, just for the laughs we got.

Howard and David Bellamy were two brothers from Brown County, Florida. They had a significant hit record called *Let Your Love Flow,* written by another roadie friend named Larry Williams.

Larry and Sam Cole were two of the road crew I worked with on the Neil Diamond Show before being fired from the gig. Larry wrote the song when he was the night shift manager at Royal Cartage, where he and Sam Cole delivered band gear to the studios. The three of them and Jim Cantale eventually became the Neil Diamond stage crew.

Howard was the laid back easy going weed smoking brother. Howard loved his pot. He favored a unique strain he called "rattler," as in rattlesnake. You could tell him anything, and he'd react nonchalantly and take it in stride.

David had a massive but well managed low-key ego. He came-on with an air of cool and pseudo sultry. "Hey… I'm David Bellamy." He was a country version of *Arthur "The Fonz" Fonzarelli* from the TV show *Happy Days*.

David always found a way to jam me up with silly, illogical things.

He might say, "I want my guitars over there." I'd say, "David, you're on the other side of the stage. Do you really want to walk all the way across the stage to change guitars?"

The Scotti Brothers managed The Bellamy's. One of the Scotti's of lesser stature traveled with the group at times. He was "the heavy." If a situation required a little "weight" behind it, he went in and "straightened it out." Like when crew meals were late, he'd go into the club owner and say, "Hey, where's the food? Let's go. Get the food here. My guys gotta eat."

A truck driver with the Bellamy's once showed up high on some sort of downers. He kept trying to get in the truck to drive to the next gig. Clearly stoned out of his mind, the guy was so ripped he was barely standing on his own, stumbling and weaving all over the place. When I tried to get the truck keys away from him, he kept pushing me away. That turned into a shoving match that resulted in my taking a full swing at him and knocking him out, much to the shock of David Bellamy, the leader of the group. David and I disagreed, but I think I saved the guys life.

I still sent him home and replaced him.

The Bellamy Brothers took any gig that was offered them, anywhere, anytime. When I went to Europe with them, I was in a little European box truck you could barely stand up in. Driving in Europe is a pain-in-the-butt. Have you ever seen a road map of Germany? Before GPS, if you wanted to try out a new guy, you could take him to Germany and give him a roadmap. If he figured it out, if he could get you from points A to B, he got the job as far as I'm concerned.

"We were doing clubs, little stinky clubs. We played a club that had a tin floor...a tin floor! It was stupid, but the brothers played it. We must have played every dive club in Europe."

Once, in a hotel in Germany with the Bellamy's, I walked down a hallway on the twelfth floor. The Drummer got off the elevator carrying a massive painting in a fancy wooden frame that was as tall as he was.

"Where are you going with that," I said,

"I want to show it to The Bellamy's."

Nobody on tour ever differentiated between the two brothers. They rarely referred to them as Howard or David. It was as if they were one entity, *The Bellamy's*.

David and Howard were on the phone talking to the US about upcoming dates, and I was on my way to join them, so I said, "I'll walk with you."

The Drummer walked right into David's room, past both brothers, out on to their balcony. He threw the painting over the railing and onto the roof of the glass-enclosed restaurant 12 floors below. It landed with a loud crash on the glass roof above the diners. Everyone in the restaurant scattered. They thought they were in the war again.

That guy was always a problem. I had to bail him out of jail once right before a show after he'd been arrested for vagrancy.

Another time in Europe, we were all on an escalator. Several men in tactical gear brandishing assault weapons were waiting at the bottom. They scanned the descending crowd. I've never been so scared in my life. I didn't know if they were there for us or not. It scared us all, and I thought to myself, "Now what... Protecting them from gunmen isn't exactly in my job description. I wear a lot of hats with these guys, but I don't wear that kind of hat."

I turned to Howard, standing behind me because he was always stoned, and said, "You better straighten out, pass it along." We stepped off the escalator and walked past the gunmen like altar boys following their vicar in a holy day procession.

Back in the US on The Bellamy's tour bus, we drove down the road to the next gig on a Texas tour. Howard spotted a steak house that was part of a cattle auction. We were all hungry, but Howard was always hungry, mainly because he was always stoned. "It has to be a good place to eat," he said. "It's part of a cattle auction."

We pulled in and parked the bus. It's hard to hide a bus; it announces your arrival. And arrive we did. With me leading the pack like a drum major, we filed in expecting to be shown to a table. Instead, we waited, gathered in a clump at the door, waiting to be ushered in. The place was packed with cowboys, real cowboys with boots and hats, and everything. We stood there like fenceposts until a waitress came over and said bluntly, "You can't eat here."

"Excuse me," I said. "We can't eat here? Why?"

"Why? Because you've got a nigger with you," nodding toward the black Drummer.

I mumbled to myself, "Oh no. I can't believe this." Then I turned to Howard and said, "Howard, don't say a word. We're kind of outnumbered here."

"Back on the bus," I groused, "Let's go."

As everyone turned to leave, the waitress said in her Texas drawl, "I can get you something to go, but you ain't bringing that nigger in here."

We were starving, and we didn't have time to stop again. Each stop wasted precious time. I'd have to round the guys up and get them back on the bus all over again. I needed to get the show back on the road. We still had a lot of miles to cover.

The waitress offered me a list of dinner options. I chose a steak dinner and said, "I'll take six of those."

Then she snapped, "Go around the back. Someone will meet you there with the bill and the dinners." She had humiliated us and added insult to injury by making us go to the back door to pick up the meals.

I marched back to the bus, my arms full of Styrofoam dinner boxes, and passed them out growling, "They're all the same, you get what you get."

For the next hundred miles, I listened to a band full of stoners crowing like banty roosters about how they should have held their ground. They'd all been passive little lambs when they were stoned and hungry and face to face with a sea of cowboy hats with real cowboys in them, now they were full of fight. I stood up and said, "Hey, I can turn the bus around if you want to go back and fight." No one said a word.

So much for standing their ground.

I was in the hotel coffee shop one-morning eating breakfast on another Bellamy's tour date in Chicago. A crewman rushed frantically over to my table and, in a serious low tone, said, "The Truck is missing."

Thinking he was kidding, I said, "Leave me alone, I'm eating my breakfast."

"I'm serious," he said, "it's gone missing."

24

"If I get up from this table and you're joking, someone's going to die," I said.

I was starting to get that this was no joke and followed him outside to where the truck and bus were parked back to back the night before. Sure enough, the bus was where we'd left it, but there was a colossal empty space where the truck had been. Instead of stealing a random amp or a valuable instrument, thieves had jacked the entire truck. It turned out to be a new trend in rock n roll. Thieves located tour trucks parked overnight. Instead of fooling around with penny-ante heists of a random guitar or an amp, they'd steal the entire truck full of gear worth thousands of dollars.

One holiday Toni and I were invited over to David Bellamy's house. David and his wife, Toni and I, and Howard and his girlfriend partied for three days. We never left the house. I don't think we ate a complete meal during that time either.

On the Bellamy's last Las Vegas show at the Golden Nugget, I was done with Vegas. As a closing night prank, I went out on stage and filled Howard's cowboy boot with whipped cream during the show. The group was never going back to the Nugget. "They were done, I was done, we were all done."

Then They fired me in Europe.

The Brothers were prostituting themselves in Europe. I was hauling the gear around in another small euro-truck setting up and breaking it down, loading the truck, and doing whatever the band needed to be done, like babysitting the stoner brother! I'd set up, and The Bellamy's would do a couple of shows a night then move on to the next toilet of a joint. I'd load out practically in the middle of the night then drive some insane distance to the next one while trying to read a Michelin map. I was getting beat-up, and my nerves were at the ragged edge.

The last straw for me was when a club owner got on me for breaking down the gear while there were still dancers on the floor. I had a slight chance of getting a few hours' sleep in the next city if I got out of there quickly and got on the road.

Club owners are the same all over the world. They're not in the entertainment business. They are in the business of selling alcohol. Bands are just glorified sign-spinners that draw the patrons to the drinks. They couldn't care less if I fell asleep at the wheel and ended up wrapped around a telephone pole or a bridge abutment.

That owner would just not get out of my face. We ended up in a heated argument. He couldn't or wouldn't get-it and kept screaming at me. I'd been very patient and considerate of his customers as I rolled my cases to the door. Still, I'd had enough of his Nazi-like authoritarian "You will obey me" crap, and I told him to stick his dance floor and his patrons where the sun doesn't shine because I had to get on the road.

Then the stoner brother came up and let me know his big bro was pissed that I had spoken to the club owner in that way. He and I were always on good terms; after all, it was me that kept him from being popped by the local gendarmes and made sure he stood up (and looked) straight. He said he'd talk to his brother, but it was already too late. Big Bro jumped right in where the club owner left off and screamed, "You don't talk to the club owners like that." By then, I had taken enough flak from all sides, and I told him to stuff it too. That's when he fired me.

"Fine," I barked. "Since I don't work for you, I don't have to load this truck, and I don't have to drive it to the next gig either. You can do that yourself. And thanks for your support." Then as he stormed off, the little brother said something like, "He doesn't really mean it. He'll apologize."

"I'm standing right here," the attitude in my voice replied. But big bro never came back. I went back to the hotel, sat down, and thought, "What have I done…"

There would be no apology, and I knew it. My time with the Bellamy's had ended, and at that point, I just didn't care.

4

Azoff: A common Thread

I was carrying an amp across a stage. There was this little pain-in-the-ass guy, standing center-stage, right in my way.

"HEY…" I shouted, "get outta my way."

Offstage, my wife Toni's girlfriend whispered to her,

"Do you know who that it is?"

"No, who is he," she answered irreverently.

"My God," She said… "It's Irving Azoff!"

"So what…"

"It's Irving Azoff, the Eagles manager, that's what!"

Toni was not going to be impressed, "He should probably get out of the way and let the crew do their work," Toni answered. "Before somebody drops something on his fancy loafers and ruins his day."

In the beginnings of rock n roll in the 1960s, the rock n roll universe was a dark void. Out of the void, a young soon to be god of the entertainment business exploded into being. A medical student from Danville, Illinois, the twenty-two-year-old was not a musician. He couldn't play note one. But music is mathematics, and he knew how to do math. He could do numbers in his head, and everything he saw in the world of live music added up to big numbers. Big numbers with dollar signs in front of them.

By his late teens, Irving Azoff had handled promotion for a dozen local bands. Then he landed a job promoting a string of college type clubs in the Midwest. Eventually, he found himself booking acts in five states, from up-coming artists like the Buckingham's and the Crying Shames, to the James Gang and REO Speedwagon.

In 1973 Irving ran into Joe Walsh playing a solo weekday gig at the Whiskey A-Go-Go on the Sunset Strip in LA. They knew each other from when Joe was the guitarist with the James Gang. Joe admitted that things hadn't been going well for him. Azoff responded that it wasn't his playing but his management. "With proper management," he said, "you could be a star."

The next day Joe signed with Irving, who promised to devote every waking hour to taking charge of his affairs and getting him released from all existing contracts.

Azoff was sharing an apartment with another client, Dan Fogelberg. They knew each other from their early days in Illinois. He promised to devote his life to Fogelberg's success as he'd done with Walsh. One year later, Fogelberg had an album out on Epic, and it went gold. Joe's album that contained the hit Rocky Mountain Way also went gold. True to his promise, he had made them both stars.

Azoff was just twenty-two years old when not long after his first successes with Joe Walsh and Fogelberg, he approached David Geffen for a job. He walked right into Geffen-Roberts (Eliot Roberts) management, bypassing assistants and secretary types. Going directly to Geffen, he asked for a job.

Azoff got the job for a salary, and Geffen remembers the deal was, "His clients were now ours." The next day Azoff had access to phones, secretaries, agents, and executives. It was as if he'd been working there forever. Geffen said, "I knew he was going to be trouble from day one."

Irving had minimal contact with the Eagles at first. Then through a mix-up on the part of office staff, he finally came into full contact with them. Someone in the office had screwed up their limo pick-up at the airport, and they were stuck there and livid. Not wanting to deal with an irate Glenn Frey in his face, Eliot Roberts asked Azoff if he wouldn't mind handling it. "Tell them to get a hippie in a cab," Roberts said.

Frey came down hard on Irving: "Other labels provide limos for their artists, and we get hippies in cabs." After listening to Frey's complaints about fifteen minutes with the phone held at arm's length, Azoff assured him that everything would be taken care of. He hung up and quickly made sure a limo was immediately dispatched to them at the airport. The story goes that from then on, Roberts called on Azoff to handle the Eagles.

The band was already unhappy about *Desperado*'s failure and the problems they were having leading up to the recording of their next album. Azoff began to have thoughts of taking over full-time management of the band. He thought if he could get the Eagles, he could take them right to the top.

The Eagles had returned to England to complete their third Album with Glyn Johns. The famed record producer of such legends as The Rolling Stones, The Who, Led Zeppelin, Eric Clapton, and other giants was at the helm as producer. About midway through their scheduled time, the Eagles had only two tracks completed. It was no secret that the band, especially Glenn Frey, had differences with Johns. They fired Johns and returned to California.

It became Azoff's responsibility to deal with getting the new Eagles record completed. He suggested Bill Szymczyk, a producer he intended to use for REO Speedwagon. He was banking on Szymczyk's abilities to give the Eagles the harder rock sound they wanted. He arranged a meeting with them, and Szymczyk played them the masters for the Joe Walsh album he'd just completed. The band liked what they heard and were satisfied Szymczyk was someone they could work with and could give them the sound they were looking for.

They returned to the studio. When the first few tracks were finished, Azoff held meetings with Henley and Frey. They talked about the possibilities of them leaving their current management so he could devote himself to them.

According to Glenn, the first time they got with Irving, there was just something about him. He was about their age and had already made the careers of Walsh and Fogelberg. They all seemed to be positioned to rise to the top at the same time and decided that Irving Azoff was the guy that could make it happen.

As previous management dissolved, it was evident to Frey and Henley how little real money they had actually made. They called a meeting with David Geffen and unloaded both barrels, Don and Glenn. By the time they'd finished their verbal assault Geffen, and Roberts wished them the best of luck and released them of all obligations to management. Then Frey and Henley contacted Azoff to let him know that they were free and clear and ready to sign with him if he was still committed.

Azoff complained to Geffen and Roberts about what he thought were "unfulfilled compensation promises" to the band. Now he had a reason to make his break as well, and he did.

Don Henley called Roberts and Geffen out on being the Eagles managers *and* their record label, which constituted a conflict of interest right from the start. When both the label and management were downsized, the band was out on the streets. Luckily, Irving was there for them. And nobody messed with Irving.

5

The Eagles: Riding the Ride

In early 1980 I was touring with the band REO Speedwagon when they opened for the Eagles. I got on well with the Eagles crew during load-in, load out, and the changeover between acts. We got on so well they offered me a job with the tour. The Eagles crew needed a man to help with load-ins, load out's, and to take care of Glenn and his many guitars, both on and off stage. I immediately pounced on the opportunity.

On my first tour with The Eagles, I quickly figured out that the 80's version, much like the band Steely Dan, consisted of two principals, Don Henley and Glenn Frey. The others, exceptional in their own right, were supplemental players, outstanding players, not just "sidemen." But not the core of the group and the decision-making process, either creatively or in business.

They were like the Henley-Frey brothers. "They were the guys. What they said went, and whatever they wanted, they got."

Early on in their careers, Henley and Frey even lived together. They wrote songs together, partied together, and they chased women together.

Like every partnership, there was a Felix and an Oscar. Henley was definitely the Felix, and Glenn was a pretty good candidate for Oscar. But in their case, Eagle Oscar was always on time or early, and Eagle Felix was still late. As for an anal-retentive side, Eagle Felix was right to type. Yet, for the most part, they kept things pretty simple and down to earth.

The third principle in the group was manager and Hollywood mogul Irving Azoff. Nothing in the Eagles got done, and nothing was decided without the approval of the big three. Among Eagles, Don and Glenn were "the gods," but Irving was the Supreme Being.

I was not a big fan of the band in their early days. But as they evolved, I liked them more and more. When I got the job, I quickly learned the history of the group. I'd heard stories of how the early Eagles were the backup band for Linda Ronstadt. They left Ronstadt with big ideas and vowed they'd never be sidemen again. Maybe that's why they treated and paid the other guys on stage so well. Their talents as journeymen and craftsmen were highly valued, though, as just part of the band. But as a group, they didn't always agree with one another and frequently squabbled amongst themselves.

We on the crew had always heard that Felder was never happy. There were selfish attitudes and behaviors we got from him towards us that seemed to back up the stories. He wasn't the crew's favorite Eagle, though he did have one of us assigned to take care of him and his guitars. Like the rest of us on the stage crew, he worked for the corporate entity "The Eagles," not the individual we looked after on stage. But his guy Jimmy Collins was as dedicated and as loyal to him as the rest of us were to our guys. We were professionals.

My guy Glenn was on stage-right along with Timothy B. Schmidt. I'd never known Timothy to want a change of strings on his bass. But I was responsible for his set-up and his spare bass as well. Timothy was easy. The only thing I had to do for Timothy was to make sure his wife off in the wings had a cigarette. I was glad Timothy was easy. Glenn kept me hopping all night long. With all the guitar changes and re-tuning, we did during the show, we kept busy for the entire show. We looked out for each other as well and covered for each other when it was necessary. When a piece of gear broke down or came unplugged, we were called onstage during the show to fix it. The rest of the time, we lurked in the shadows behind the amp line and beyond the lights like film noir private eyes tailing their man. We kept a cat-like focus on them, anticipating the next instrument change or an onstage mishap that required our attention.

All in all, between us on the stage crew, we had about forty guitars to tune each night. We thanked God for Ernie Ball, the string manufacturer that endorsed the band. They kept us stocked up with an endless supply, an entire road case of every possible gauge string we could ever need, or our guys could ever want.

At center stage, Henley had his guy Tony Taibi. Tony set up his drums and tuned and maintained them. Rock n roll drum kits are manually operated beat machines with a lot of moving parts. They require constant maintenance and loads of TLC. Most drummers and their techs are like mechanics with hardware stores. They're always changing heads, tweaking, re-configuring, or repairing their kits.

When Joe Vitale was with the show, Tony took care of his drum kit as well.

On stage left, Jimmy Collins looked after Don Felder, and a three-fingered guitar tech by the name of Jage Jackson took care of Joe Walsh. Jage did a fantastic job. He could tune Joe's guitars and maintain Joe's rig to perfection despite his handicap, and Joe loved him. He took care of the keyboards as well.

I was a proud member of the Eagles stage crew. We took care of each artist's needs on stage. There was also a production manager and a couple of tour managers who kept the entire tour together. Additionally, sound engineers, riggers, bus drivers, truck drivers, and a wardrobe person made up the overall crew.

We were seasoned veterans of numerous rock n roll tours. We worked together well on the assembly and production line of a movable music factory. We erected our plant in a different city every day, then tore it down at the end of a production run, packed it in trucks, and moved it from city to city, across the country, or around the world. Then we built it again, over and over, in city after city.

Young fans look at roadies, or stage techs as we were called, and think we live a glamorous lifestyle hanging-out backstage with their idols. But some of us had a saying, "It ain't easy being us." It was a two-edged sword. We said it sarcastically on rare days off lounging poolside at a 5-star hotel or traveling to Europe or Japan. In those circumstances, it was the best job in the world that gave us a sense of freedom and adventure you don't get in a day job.

But on long loadouts, and even longer bus rides, or on days when we showed up with little sleep and nothing seemed to go right, or the trucks were late through no fault of their own, it really wasn't easy being us. Some days, the hundreds of little details, the months of planning, and the hours of hard physical work that go into the production of a rock n roll tour, just don't sync up for one reason or another. But as Rolling Stones Keith Richards and Mick Jagger said, "It's only rock n roll, but I like it."

I hadn't been with the band long, a few weeks, maybe. I was standing in my spot in the shadows behind the amp line between cues and guitar changes. Suddenly Glenn began to wander aimlessly in the dark heading unfocussed toward the back of the stage. I just happened to turn around as he neared the back edge, where it was a long drop to the arena floor. Out of pure instinct, I turned at the exact right time and reacted by sticking my arm out. I got him in my grasp and guided him back to his spot, and off the dangerous path he was on. A backstage guest of the band that night shouted out, "Nice catch!" It was Dallas Cowboys cornerback Mel Renfro.

If I'd have missed Glenn, he would have taken a long dive off the stage and hit the concrete floor with an impact that might have resulted in one or more severe injuries and possibly ended his musical career.

It had been known to happen. In the early days when roadies were called roadies and not professional "stage techs." The gear and the rock n roll stagecraft were still pretty primitive.

Whenever a bunch of roadies got together to swap stories, we would often tell of the rock stars we'd known that had literally stepped off the stage in the dark where the lighting ended. Several rock stars had been seriously injured in those early days.

Later, I found out that someone backstage had given Glenn something that should have just given him a "buzz." He must have taken a bit too much of whatever it was. It had given him way too much "buzz" and not enough focus. It caused him to be totally disoriented and entirely out of it.

The show that night was the end of the tour, and we were all traveling back to LA on the band's chartered jet. When the plane reached cruising altitude, I was snugly in my seat, looking forward to a comfy ride home when one of the road managers came back and said, "Glenn wants to see you."

Glenn's near mishap was long forgotten. I thought, "Uh-Oh," What did I do now? I could be going home without a job. I got up and ambled toward the front of the plane, ready to take my lumps. When I got to Glenn's seat, he handed me an envelope. It was one of the Eagles tour logo envelopes our per diem came in. As he gave it to me, he looked up and said, "Thanks, you saved my life, and I wanted you to know that I appreciate it." "No worries," I said, "I'm just glad I was there at the right time. Thanks, boss."

I got back to my seat and took a closer look at the envelope.

The blank lines were filled in with *Norton,* No.: *1*, Date: Dallas *June 21, '80,* Period: *Crazy,* No. of days: *Who Knows,* Amount due: *$500*. Reason: *NICE CATCH*. The boss had bonused me $500.

It was the beginning of a long beautiful friendship and a great working relationship.

6

Read Your Itinerary

I yawned and stretched then rolled over beneath the covers. My eyes opened, and I realized I was in my bunk on the crew bus in the middle of a tour. Half-awake, I bus-surfed my way down the aisle, groggy and grumpy, making my way toward the smell of fresh-brewed coffee.

The new guy stuck his head out of the curtain of his lower bunk and mumbled, "What day is it? … Where are we?"

Balancing myself against the bunks with outstretched hands, I kept walking. Smirking and grumbling half under my breath and loud enough to be heard, I said, "Read your Itinerary, numbnuts! Who do I look like? Alex Trebek?"

"Never mess with me first thing in the morning on tour before I've had my coffee. And I don't play twenty questions. So, if you're smart, you'll learn to read your itinerary if you need to know where you are or where the next show is."

Another head popped out of a bunk and said with maximum sarcasm, "This guy's so green he wouldn't burn. What are you? New? Oh yeah, I forgot, you are!"

I poured myself a cup and took my first sip toward becoming human again. Then I stared blankly, long and hard down the aisle until the life forces began to course through my body and the fog started to lift.

"I've got one word for him," I said; "Acetone!"

That got a chuckle out of the guy with his head still hung out between the bunk curtains. "Acetone," he agreed, with a wicked smile.

The kid *was* new, and he *was* delusional. Because he was the brother of one of the band, he had the mistaken idea that he was immune to carrying his weight on tour. He was not on the tour because of a royal bloodline or his expertise in stagecraft. He was there because it was time for him to step up to the plate and score some hits of his own, and Glenn knew it.

Many tour days on a bus began with a little rap on the side of my bunk. Then a hand parted the curtain and nudged me until I stirred. It was the production manager's way of easing me into the day. I was the only one of the stage crew needed at the beginning of every load in. My job was to set the stage risers. It had to be done as soon as the stage was placed. The stage platform was the first thing that had to happen when the hall was opened. Then the local crew rallied at the loading dock, and the first truck door was cracked.

I always acknowledged that I was awake with an assortment of grunts and groans that let him know I was up and ready to report for duty. Then I'd slide out of my bunk in my pajamas and wriggle into my robe and slippers. I'd make my way to the stage dressed just like that, in my bus uniform, and gather my stagehands for the first task of the day.

"Listen up," I'd say. "My name is Norton. And all of you guys are called Tommy. When I need something, I'm going to call out, 'Hey Tommy,' and one of you guys needs to be right here in front of me."

Then, with the help of a few of the local stagehands, I'd set my risers. When I was done, I'd go back to my bunk and get a little more sleep or just lie there quietly until the riggers, and the sound and lights guys were far enough along in their set up that the stage crew could load in the band gear.

Glenn loved his brother. But at that time, he was "still maturing," shall we say. When we were off the road, and Glenn was out of town, he called me to have me gently "evacuate" his brother from the premises of his home in the Hollywood Hills. He thought his brother was acting irresponsibly by squatting in his home while he was gone. Ya think?

Glenn lived in a beautiful place in the Hollywood Hills. He was proud of his beautiful home, and he really did love his brother. But having Matt always underfoot and unannounced was cramping his style.

I'd go over to the house to deliver the news, and somehow, he'd spot me coming and hide. Then I'd track him down and say, "You gotta leave. If you're still here when your brother gets home, I'm outta work. So, guess what? You're outta *here*." Then Glenn would come back a week later and feel sorry for him and bring the kid back.

A solution to the brother's situation came when Glenn said, "Take him on the road with you. Put him to work." Apparently, Glenn thought a little hard work would make a man out of him. But the kid had not even a clue. In many ways, he was less than useless, just taking up space on the crew bus.

I put him to work doing all the simple stupid jobs like putting the front case covers on the amps...all the shitty jobs, like cleaning the Marley stage cover with acetone. Marley is a brand name for a rubberized linoleum initially developed as a stage covering for dancers because it looks good, it's non-slip, and provides a good looking even finish to a stage that looks great when lit.

As good as it looks, it still gets the occasional spills or streak marks, and cleaning Marley with acetone is a pretty nasty business.

"It stinks," he said.

"Yeah, it stinks," I answered. "You wanted to come on the road, you're on the road! Use the acetone!"

Then he went to his brother. "He made me do the whole stage in acetone." Glenn came to me and asked, "What did he do, what happened?" I replied that the kid was hungover from the night before. "I just made him do the acetone, nobody *wants* to do acetone, but it has to be done."

Glenn's response was, "Good job!"

He may have been trying to make a man out of the kid, but I think he was also just sick of his brother breaking into his house when he wasn't there.

Later after he got the hang of using the acetone and learned to live with it, he got a little cocky. It's a typical syndrome of show biz relatives on the road. All of a sudden, he was one of the band. He wanted to ride on the band bus. "I'm gonna ride with my brother," he said one night. "No, no, no, you're not," I said. "You're on the crew, you ride with the crew or not at all. The band doesn't want you there."

On the first day on the bus, we gave him "the" speech. The one every roadie knows by heart: "You don't poop in the bus toilet, you got that? No pooping on the bus…it's just not done!"

Every road dog who has ever ridden the crew bus knows there is always a bunk reserved for hand luggage and other carry-ons. "We made Matt sleep in it," with all the bags piled up at the foot of the bunk. Think of it as a rite of passage, tough love. Every time he whined, I repeated, "You wanted to be on the road… you're on the road!"

One night we left New York and stopped in a truck stop for fuel. Truck stops are always impressive on the road. We did the usual late-night prowl around the convenience store, most of the guys in typical post-show bus outfits of shorts, t-shirts, flip flops, and caps to keep the common affliction of bus-hair at bay.

While the driver fueled-up the bus, we browsed typical offerings of truck friendly 12-volt DC products like TVs and coffee makers, as well as trucking hardware, road atlases, tools, knives, and other odd items of interest to truckers. Then we purchased a wide assortment of junk food snacks for the road.

We all piled back onto the bus and took off again down the highway. A few miles down the road, someone said, "Hey, where's Jimmy?" We took a headcount, then checked the bunks and the toilet. There was no Jimmy. They all looked at me. "I don't know," I said. "It wasn't my turn to watch him." Then I went to the driver. "Did you see Jimmy get back on the bus?" He replied simply, "Nope."

"Turn the bus around. We have to go back," I said.

Luckily Twenty minutes later, we found him waiting patiently at the truck stop. It turns out Jimmy had taken a prescription sleeping medication that most likely kicked in while he was browsing. He may have forgotten he had a bus to catch.

On another tour, we stopped for gas and once again piled off the bus while the bus driver fueled-up. We did our usual rounds of the convenience store, got our snacks, and returned to the bus. Once again, we did a headcount and came up short. One of the lighting crew was missing. This time we organized a search party, a roadie posse. Everyone went out in a different direction and scoured the Truckstop looking for him. We found him a short while later and piled back on the bus. "But I was pissed." I cornered the guy and said, "If I ever have to waste time looking for you again, I'm gonna leave you there!"

Some road crews call that getting the "grease spot." It's what you find when you show up late, and the bus is gone, all except the oil spot where it was parked.

Even worse is traveling with the band. Musicians tend to wander off in all directions with no sense of time. Just when you think you've got them all on the bus, one goes missing. Then you go out searching for them. You find them and get back on the bus only to find that someone else is AWOL. It's like herding cats, or kindergarteners on a trip to the zoo, without the name tags pinned to their shirts and the hand holding in a single file line.

When you finally corral them, you might say, "Please, just sit, I only have one more to find. Of course, some take it as 'Sit, roll over, fetch!' Some musicians just plain refuse to take direction and are defiant and ignore everything you say. You can't win."

7

Glenn and Me

In 1972 Cameron Crowe was working at a local underground paper in San Diego. He and a photographer friend went to see the Eagles in concert. "Take It Easy" was a big hit. Their plan was to sneak backstage and get an interview with the band. He liked that they were strong on vocals and stronger on attitude. They talked their way backstage, and the road manager put them in a room with the original band. Glenn Frey was not in the room, but every other sentence was about Glenn. Glenn Did this, Glenn did that, and then Glenn… When the door next opened, Glenn Frey walked in with a notable Detroit attitude. Crowe thought of him as part musician, part tactician, and part comedian, and someone who knew the big picture

I was Glenn's guy, both onstage and off. He kept me on a retainer, and I was always on call. Most tasks he gave me were routine, but some ended up being interesting or funny in one way or another.

We were between tours at home in LA when Glenn called. He wanted me at his house in the canyon as soon as possible. I was in my car in a matter of minutes, making the forty-five-minute drive into LA from my home in Palmdale. But when the boss called, I ran. No one else had ever had me on a retainer before, and I was thankful for that. But I earned every penny of it.

When I got to the house, he said, "We're going downtown. I want to buy a mannequin."

"OK," I said cautiously, but thought to myself, "What the heck does he want with a mannequin?"

We braved the traffic and made the drive downtown in his Camaro and searched for the mannequin store, then eventually found it.

"We walked into the mannequin joint together and Glenn immediately said to the clerk, 'I want to buy a mannequin.'"

The clerk says, "Sure, no problem. Do You want a life-size man, woman, or child? We have them all, whatever you need."

Glenn takes a look around then spots a female in a sitting down pose with her hands out like she's playing the piano. He makes the purchase and says to me, "Load that one in the Camaro."

The Camaro was a small car and a hardtop, and I couldn't get the mannequin to fit inside. So, I looked at Glenn and said, "It ain't gonna go, boss. What do you want me to do?"

Glenn looks at the mannequin then back at me and says soberly as a judge, "Cut the roof off."

"Cut the roof off?" I said. "I can't cut the roof off."

Now I'm cursing to myself, "This guy's got me jumping through hoops; for a friggin mannequin!"

Glenn says, "Tell the guy you'll be back in two days after you have the roof cut off."

Later I dropped Glenn off and drove the Camaro over to an auto shop run by a guy Glenn knew. I told the guy, "Glenn wants the roof cut off, and off comes the roof."

'When I took the car back to Glenn, he sent me back to the mannequin joint to pick up the mannequin. 'Make sure he helps you fit it into the front seat.'"

Back I go downtown, into the deepest darkest part of the intestinal tract of the city. I tell the mannequin guy, "Put the mannequin in the front seat." He puts it snugly into the passenger seat, and I left thinking, "Why am I driving all the way across town with a damn naked female mannequin in the front seat? This is ridicules."

I drove across town from downtown LA on surface streets. Wilshire Blvd. to Vermont and up through Korea town, then Across Sunset Blvd, and up into the Hollywood Hills, heading back to Glenn's house in the canyon with a naked female mannequin in the front seat of a Camaro with the top chopped off.

The mannequin was posed, staring straight ahead with her right arm on the windowsill. When I stopped at a light, a cop glanced over at me then looked away. The cop looked back, directly at me this time, and said, "Who's that?" Me being a smart-ass from Jersey, I said, "That's my mother."

The cop burst out laughing, "What are you doing with that mannequin?"

I answered, "That's not a mannequin; that's my mother, and I'm taking her home." "Only in LA," I imagine him thinking as he pulled away, chuckling and shaking his head.

I had just driven across the entire city from downtown and up into the Hollywood Hills through traffic on surface streets, stopping for lights and getting gawked at the whole way to Glenn's house. I pulled in the driveway, walked into the house, and handed him the keys.

"Here's the keys to the Camaro, and your mannequin."

"Mannequin?" he said. "What mannequin?"

The mannequin you had me pick-up from downtown and drive all the way across the city in your chopped-top Camaro.

"I didn't have you drive any mannequin."

"Go outside and look," I said. "It's sitting in the front seat."

Outside Glenn laughed. He had played me like his favorite guitar. He hadn't really cared too much about the mannequin, but I had been punked big time.

Glenn had gotten me to do something stupid and had a good laugh. It really was stupid, and I fell for it hook line and sinker. Then I laughed too. But the mannequin really did have a purpose. Some people keep their TV on when they're home alone to keep them company. Glenn had his dummy.

Cameron Crowe was right; Glenn was part musician, part tactician, and part stand-up comic. I'd add prankster to that list as well.

Glenn produced an act together with legendary producer Jerry Wexler. Wexler was responsible for coining the term "rhythm and blues." R&B became the new title for African American music, initially called "Race Music back then."

One day Glenn called me from Texas, where he and Wexler were putting finishing touches on the artist's album. He said, "I need you to go to the airport and pick up the artist. I sent her to LA to buy some clothes for the album cover. I want you to take her out shopping."

Palmdale was a long hike into the city, so I told Toni, "I have to go into town and pick up this girl singer from Texas that Glenn is producing. He wants me to take her clothes shopping in Hollywood because she has nothing, and he wants her to look good on the album cover."

I had no idea what she even looked like when I arrived at the airport. Somehow, we connected, and I Introduced myself.

"Hi, I'm Bobby Thompson. I work for Glenn. Everybody calls me Norton."

"Oh… You're Norton. I've heard so many stories about you."

"Good, Good, I hope. I'm taking you to the hotel to get you checked in. Then I'm Going to take you shopping on Glenn."

She was excited, and in a bubbly voice, replied, "OK, no problem."

We pulled in to L'Ermitage, one of the most exclusive hotels in the world. I turned to her and said, "Get checked in, take a shower, relax, do what you have to do, and I'll pick you up in the morning."

"Oh no," she said, "I'm going to throw these bags in the room, and I'll be ready to go. We're going now."

I'm thinking, "OK… there goes my day. I better call Toni and let her know I may not be home today. I may not be home forever!"

Jim Shea, a well-known celebrity photographer in Hollywood, gave me a few tips on elegant shops I could take her to. We showed up at the first shop, a swanky lingerie shop you had to press a button to get into. We go in, and she's walking around trying on a few things. "She looks at this, and she looks at that, then she tries on a nightgown, a hundred and fifty bucks!" I was never told how much to spend, and knowing Glenn, I assumed there was no budget.

Then I said, "We have time enough for one more shop before they close for the day." So, we go down to another posh place.

"Our Texas shit kicker is walking around examining stuff when in comes this little actress, Bernadette Peters, a big star at the time." There were only three people in the store beside the sales lady; The artist, Bernadette Peters, and me. Miss Texas begins picking up items and holding them up for the sales lady to see. "How much is this; how much is this?" I went over and quietly said, "It doesn't matter how much it is. If you like it, buy it. Whatever you want you got it." (In my mind I'm thinking, "So we can get out of here.")

We walked around while she browsed, and I think, "*I'll probably never see Toni again*." Then she picks up a sweater, a cashmere sweater, and turns to me. "This is a beautiful sweater, isn't it?"

"Yeah," I agreed sarcastically, "beautiful."

"How much is this sweater," she says to me.

"I honestly don't have a clue," I said, then turned to the salesperson. Excuse me, ma'am, how much is this sweater.

"Twelve hundred dollars," she answered cheerfully.

Then Miss Texas, without missing a beat, looks at the salesperson and says. "What's this made of, pussy hair?"

Bernadette Peters subtly took note, then wisely and quietly began to work her way to the front of the store and out the door.

I looked over at Miss Texas and said, "You have to be cool; you can't say things like that in public anymore."

With a sense of righteous indignity, she snapped back, "What, what's wrong with that?"

"What's wrong with that," I said, "is that you're in the public eye now. You're on the verge of a career that is everything you ever dreamed of; you'll get killed for stuff like that."

Then I thought, "We're done, time to eat. I announced that we'd meet Toni at a steakhouse I knew of for a nice dinner.

At dinner, she let it all out. "She started out with a steady stream of Fuck this and Fuck that… at a high decibel level." The term potty mouth would have been gentle and overly generous. Her ability to express herself with expletives was overshadowed only by her lack of inhibition in using them in public and social situations. I don't know where she came from in Texas, but I think the term shit-kicker says it all.

We somehow made it through dinner without being ejected from what I considered an upscale LA restaurant. Toni mentioned she had to get home to take care of our daughter. Miss Texas had other ideas.

"Let's go out dancing. There must be someplace in this 'hick town' we can go to. Take me to one of those fancy clubs y'all talk about."

I rolled my eyes at Toni and said, "I gotta stay with her to get her back to the hotel where I can lock her in her room for the night with a guard so she can't escape."

"Go home, Toni," I said. "This could get ugly."

No sooner had Toni walked away than Miss Texas started in on me. She was brimming with energy, bouncing around like fleas on a hot plate. "Where we gonna go," she said, "where we goin!"

I took her to the Whiskey A-Go-Go, the Roxy, and then The Rainbow Room. She'd approach random men and ask, "Are you a movie star? Rock Star? Singer? What do you do? What's your gig?"

I'm thinking, "What the hell is she doing."

She could have been the poster girl for drunken public behavior. "Hick town? I got your hick town lady! Where'd you leave your turnip truck, Ellie May."

Then I said, "We gotta get going. You've got a big day ahead of you tomorrow."

I got her back to her swanky digs at L'Ermitage and into her room. Then I grabbed the doorman, concierge, whatever, and said, "If that girl leaves the room for any reason, you call me. If she goes anywhere, I need to know… here's my phone number. I wrote it in letters four inches high."

I started to head up to Glenn's for the night to eliminate the long drive back to Palmdale. Then I remembered she was in a two-bedroom suite separated by a living room of sorts. I decided to camp out there for the night.

I tried to get her to buy clothes, but nothing seemed to register with her, so I called Glenn to let him know.

"Just get her on the first flight out of there," he said. "Send her back to us."

She got the big idea that she'd like to spend the day at my house because she liked Toni. I drove all the way back to Palmdale, and she spent the day with Toni and me and our teenage daughter Summer.

The next day I drove her to the airport. We parked the car, and I walked her to the terminal, checked her luggage at the curb, then got her seat assignment at the counter like I'd done for countless rock stars on tour in the past. Then I asked, "Can you find your way to the gate OK?" She said she could, and we parted ways. I breathed a sigh of relief, thinking how glad I was to be rid of her. She was a real piece of work.

In my opinion, when the Goose lays a Golden egg in your lap, indulge him. You may find it worth your while. Miss Texas was briefly with Asylum Records and other lesser blues labels. The Frey and Wexler album got great reviews but flopped, and I never heard of her again. "She'd only been on the mountain for a cup of tea."

8

Sportacus

Glenn Frey was a sports guy. So much so that he was known to certain friends as "Sportacus." He had tickets to most of the professional sporting events in LA. His seats would be a dream come true to fans and scalpers alike.

Glenn's LA Lakers basketball tickets were at floor level near the Laker bench, next to where the legendary Magic Johnson sat. "Supreme Being" Irving Azoff, merely held two seats under the backboard at floor level. As far as Laker tickets were concerned, you could go no higher in the hierarchy of Hollywood Royalty for proximity to Laker's action. Glenn's seats were on the same level as the top movers and shakers and deal makers. On that level, only legendary artists of the industry, like Denzel Washington, Dustin Hoffman, Jack Nicholson, and Leonardo DiCaprio, had seats. They sat amongst their peers from the top levels of the elite of movie, music executives, and Hollywood agents.

Even Lakers owners can't get seats at that level without the significant wheeling and dealing, political maneuvering, and deal-making that everyone else employed to get their own seats. Jack Nicholson once said about who would get his seats when he died, "The highest bidder."

Glenn was also a big Hockey Fan and had comparable season seats for the LA Kings. Hockey was a big part of Glenn's vocabulary as well. If you screwed up, you were warned that you were either in danger of being "taken off the ice," or that you *were* "off the ice."

When Glenn was really pissed at you, he would either say, "Get away from me" or, "You're off the ice." Nobody wanted to be taken off the ice. It meant when you were off the ice, you were in the penalty box just like in hockey, and you had to earn your way back in again.

Glenn's other sports passion was baseball. Glenn liked to go to Dodgers games. Sometimes, to reward you, if he knew you enjoyed baseball, he would give you four Dodger seats in a great location.

With the Eagles, we organized a team made up of band and crew and friends. We played against other bands and celebrity groups and called ourselves the *Hollywood Hoovers*. We had uniforms and everything. Our logo was similar to the Hoover Vacuum Cleaner company, and our colors were red and white, as were theirs.

Glenn got hot on the idea of going to a baseball fantasy camp in Tempe, Arizona. For $2295, anyone could attend, so Glenn made plans for him and his road manager Tommy Nixon to drive to Tempe for the camp. But first, they wanted to tune up their game a bit. Neither one of them was a great player, so they asked me along. I'm no pro, but I did play ball on my high school team, and I did pretty well.

Glenn and Tommy arranged a little practice session in Balboa Park for the three of us. Practice session? More like a "Norton hits balls to Tommy and Glenn" session. I'd hit them a variety of balls: grounders, pop fly's, and pop-ups, and they'd run around and try to catch them. "I'm working hard... on my day off." But honestly, between the two of them, there wasn't one decent player.

A few days later, I was sitting at home when the phone rang. It was from Glenn.

"Pack your clothes, you're going with us."

"Going where?" I said.

"You're going to the baseball camp with Tommy and me," Glenn answered.

So, Glenn rents a camper, and the three of us, me, Tommy Nixon, and Glenn, pile in and head for Tempe, Arizona. But first, Glenn has me pick up some music to play along the way.

Prince was a relatively new artist then. He had just come out with the song that became a big hit called 1999. Glenn kept playing it over and over again 'til it was stuck in my brain, *"Tonight*

I'm gonna party like it's 1999..." And Glenn kept saying over and over again "1999, 1999."

"We got to the camp in Tempe and Glenn was getting noticed as a celebrity and Tommy was sort of playing the big shot. But I'm playing baseball. I'm playing first base, I'm catching, I'm playing outfield."

Glenn was getting pissed because I was getting all the attention from the baseball players. They took to me because I can play baseball. "Glenn could play, sort of, but he couldn't, and Tommy Nixon couldn't play at all."

Tommy is taking Glenn to dinner every night, and I'm back at the hotel with the team guys. "They're all digging me because I can play baseball. It was great. I even got a bat from one of the Dodgers catchers."

Then all the way home, Glenn gave me shit. Shit, and more shit, really busting my chops. I said, "Glenn, I can play, I can really play. I played high school ball." He says, "Yeah, but you didn't have to show us up!" He was kind of pissed, but more in a teasing way, busting my chops. I guess his musician's ego was also a bit bruised.

Glenn may have given me crap all the way home, but I knew who he really was. He had just shelled out $2295 each for the camp, plus rooms and transportation, and we really did have a great time. It was a great example of the generosity he had always shown me. And Glenn was loyal too. If someone ever said anything against Tommy or me, Glenn would have come down on them like a ton of bricks. Apart from being my employer, he was a good friend that deserved every bit of loyalty and devotion we showed him over the years. Glenn knew how much of my time he took away from my family. He called Toni "Soul Sister, number one." Occasionally he'd send her flowers to let her know too.

Deep down, Glenn was an old-school romantic and a nice guy.

9

Winner, Winner, Chicken Dinner

If Glenn were interested in a woman romantically, he would take her out for a candlelit dinner in the quiet and romantic corner of a softly lit upscale restaurant like Dan Tana's in Hollywood, oddly enough near the Troubadour where the Eagles began. As the relationship progressed, she'd be invited for a romantic evening at his house in the canyon. At that stage, he'd supply the candles and prepare his special chicken dinner for the lucky girl.

The problem was that Glenn only knew how to cook one dish. But he had it down pat. It was a roasted chicken with little carrots and new potatoes, vegetables, and an excellent expensive wine or Champagne. I called it "the meal." Whenever Glenn was at that point in a relationship, he'd get all spun up and frantic. I'd usually get a call, and in the course of my duties for the day, he'd ask me to pick out a good chicken then remind me a hundred times, "You got the little carrots, right? What about the vegetables? And the potatoes, you got them, right?"

I always wondered what he did for an encore. On the second date, did he casually say, "How about Chinese take-out?" Did they end up sitting around in their robes eating out of little white boxes and struggling with chopsticks?

But Glenn really was an old school romantic. A mediocre cook, but a real romantic. He was a real candy and flowers, candlelit dinner, little surprise gifts of jewelry for no particular reason, kind of guy. And he actually had an appreciation for Sinatra tunes and that genre of music. In another era, he might have shown up for a girl in tie and tails for a night at the Copa Cabana and surprise her with a mink coat, flowers, a string of pearls, or a diamond bracelet.

I was at a video shoot with Glenn. He asked me to book his masseuse for after the shoot. I gave the girl a call and found that she was out of town, so I went back to Glenn to provide him with the news. One of my rules with Glenn was if anything didn't pan out, always have a solution or a suggestion before delivering the bad news. So, I said, "While you were shooting, I was talking to this girl Cindy. Aside from being a gymnast, a dancer, and a cheerleader, she does massages. Do you want me to call her?"

He answered, "Is she any good?"

With my usual Jersey sarcasm, I replied, "Well, I haven't had a massage by her, and you haven't had a massage by her either. I don't know if she's any good!"

He answered abruptly, "Call her up."

I called Cindy and said, "Hi, its Bob Thompson From the video shoot yesterday. I work for Glenn Frey. Are you available to do a massage for Glenn?"

She was available, and I made the appointment then called Glenn back with the time.

Glenn called the next day and said, as if it had never been done before, "I need your help. I invited the masseuse over. I promised I'd cook her dinner. I'm gonna cook her a chicken dinner."

"I made the 45-minute drive from Palmdale, again, and stopped at the market to fill my list. Then I went to the liquor store and picked up a bottle of Champagne. That dinner must have been great because long story short, Glenn eventually ended up marrying Cindy."

Cindy lived in a tiny apartment in the Hollywood Hills in Beachwood Canyon above Franklin Blvd with four dancer roommates during their engagement.

"None of them had a pot to piss in, and they were barely eating." "Glenn sent Cindy a twenty-five-thousand-dollar strand of pearls. At the time, it was out of character for her, given her situation. You can't eat pearls."

When Glenn found out the refrigerator was broken at the apartment, he bought her a brand-new state of the art side by side unit with all the bells and whistles available at the time. "Of course, it was on me to deliver it, another guy and me…"

We were frustrated, sweating, and struggling with this massive behemoth when Cindy's dad came up to us and said, "What are you guys doing."

Being totally Jersey again, I almost said, "picking my nose." I'm juggling a side by side refrigerator in my hands, and this guy wants to know what I'm doing. "What's it look like I'm doing… what-are-you… new?"

Then the father-in-law-to-be says, "We aren't accepting that."

"We're taking it to your daughter," I said, "It's a gift from Glenn."

"The apartment door wasn't wide enough, so we had to take the door off the hinges and shoehorn the refrigerator into the apartment until finally, we got it all the way in."

With Glenn, you always had to check out. I couldn't just go home; I had to stop at Glenn's first. He always wanted to know that everything went "cool."

At the house, he asked me how everything went. I said, "Everything went well until her father showed up and asked me what I was doing. Glenn looked at me like, "what am I getting myself into…"

Glenn and Cindy's engagement party was held at a posh resort hotel in La Quinta near Palm Springs. Glenn invited everyone he knew. He even sprang for rooms for myself and a few of us on the Eagles staff, like Tommy Nixon and me. He made a point of reminding me to be sure and bring Toni and our daughter Summer as well.

Cindy's side of the family showed up in full force. They were everywhere. In sharp contrast, Glenn only had his Mom and Dad and two brothers. But the rest of the guest list was filled out with friends and acquaintances Glenn knew from the entertainment business. One notable guest was the actor Don Johnson, famous then for his hit TV show Miami Vice. He and Glenn had recently worked together and became good friends.

For the actual wedding, Glenn bought suits for all the guys who worked for him, myself, Tommy Nixon, engineer Mike Harlow and this guy Frankie that I would eventually call Frankie The Blade that looked after his Aspen home. We all got new suits that were similar but not the same as Glenn's wedding suit.

The week before the wedding, Glenn said, "I need you to buy a truck." Sometimes I just couldn't understand some of the stuff Glenn did. I thought it a bit odd that Glenn would buy a truck

"Buy a truck," I said. Why do you want to buy a truck?

"I meant rent a truck," He answered.

"Oh, OK," I said. "That makes more sense."

I rented a truck. Glenn had me go down to this Art Deco place in Hollywood and buy a bunch of furniture to use as decorations at his Aspen house for the wedding.

"And don't forget Toni and Summer," he said, "I want them

at the wedding."

"How am I going to get them there," I said.

"You're gonna drive the truck," he answered. "We have to get furniture there."

When we finally got the truck completely loaded, it not only had the Art Deco furniture but patio furniture, cases of liquor, musical instruments, and more.

Toni and Summer and I piled into the truck for the long drive to Aspen. We knew with the three of us in the front seat facing a fourteen-hour drive, we'd need to stop somewhere about midway for the night. We found a great little hotel en route, and I asked the desk clerk for his best room.

"Well sir," the man said, "I've got a nice room with a shower, tub, and sauna in the center of the room. The shower has great lighting that changes color and everything I think you'll like it."

"I'll take it," I said,

Toni and Summer had a blast in that room. They thought it was the cat's meow and the next best thing since peanut butter. They even ordered Sushi to the room.

The next morning, we were back in the truck headed over the Rocky Mountains toward Aspen. I looked over at Summer and said, "You want to drive?" Summer's eyes got really wide with excitement, and she said, "Yeah, dad, I want to drive." Summer drove for a while and loved it. Then I got back behind the wheel and took us into Aspen.

Glenn put up all of his guests at the Jerome Hotel, a historic landmark considered the "Crown Jewell" of Aspen. Glenn got us a suite, and once again, Toni and Summer thought they died and went to heaven. But Glenn had work for me to do. He had me moving Champagne and beer cases around while Toni and Summer were hanging out at the hotel.

"I'm running back and forth for Glenn between Aspen and Snow Mass, Colorado, about twenty minutes apart. Frankie is buying and planting flowers everywhere. He said you have to drive me in the truck to pick up some flowers." Frankie couldn't drive a truck.

I said, "You can't drive a truck? How hard is it to drive a truck…? My teenage daughter can drive a truck. Are you lame? What good are you?"

There were thousands and thousands of dollars' worth of plants and flowers. Everybody had flowers, and there were flowers everywhere. It took us three days to lay out all the plants and flowers.

Toni had an awkward moment at the wedding reception:

"I saw Glenn sitting alone at a table. It was set up for about twelve people, but Glenn was sitting alone. I sat down to talk to him, and he said, 'Toni, this is for family only.' I thought he was rude because there was no reserved sign on the table, and I had no idea. In hindsight, I understood the situation. At weddings, it's traditional to have a table reserved for the bride and groom's family. What made it awkward was that there was no reserved sign and Glenn had to tell me that it was just for the family.

But I just apologized and got up and walked away."

Right before the wedding, Cindy took a dancing job in Paris for five weeks. It was vital for her to assert her independence and buy her own wedding dress. She used the money she made in France to buy a dress of her own choosing.

10

Frankie The Blade

Almost every celebrity spouse and wealthy man or woman in LA has a tennis pro, a Pilates trainer, a masseuse, or a golf instructor. They get the secret gate code to the estate and their client's cell number for their service. As a breed, they are found on the French Riviera, the Hawaiian Islands, Tahiti, the Bahamas, the spa towns of Europe, and anywhere globally, the wealthy take their leisure. They show up everywhere, private parties, movie and music premieres, product launches, art auctions, family weddings, and gatherings of their elite bosses in exotic locales across the Globe.

The perks are endless. Weekends in Aspen, flights on the jet, cruises on the yacht, and seasonal jaunts around the world. Paparazzi puzzle the identities of sun-tanned buffed out gods or goddesses with wind-blown hair, cashmere sweaters draped across their shoulders, sleeves tied loosely around their neck, following two steps behind their benefactors into a limousine, a private jet, or up a marina gangway.

Batman entrusted his loyal butler Alfred with the keys to the Bat Cave and stately Wayne Manor. Superman had Jimmy Olson. Olson sometimes temporarily took on his own superpowers to fight beside the man of steel. Kato Kaelin is always thought of as OJ's "guy" at the Rockingham Estate. In entertainment, everyone and their significant other has "a guy."

In rock n roll and music circles, "the guy" comes from either of two categories. There's "the guy" or "guys" in a posse. Or a stand-alone "guy" that comes from the same strata of life as their principal. Someone from the old neighborhood, a trusted roadie, or stage technician. He or she lives among the people and keeps their star employer in touch with their roots. A plain-speaking "guy" that tells it like it is, on retainer, available at a moment's notice. They are true friends. Employees, nonetheless, but real friends who execute their duties faithfully, loyal to the death.

The other category is "hangers-on." They have somehow endeared themselves to principals by services, disciplines, or athletic abilities, always looking for a way in or a way up.

As a loyal friend and a trail hand, I fell into the former category. I was, as I have said, "Riding the ride." I rode the trail, and I knew how the sausage was made and where it came from. I paid the dues and lived "the life." When the drive left civilization, I rode among the herd, slept in the saddle when I could, and played a part in driving the beeves to market where they were cut into steaks, or made into sausage, and delivered to the public for their pleasure and consumption.

Then there was Frankie.

Glenn's first wife was a good 'ol Texas Gal named Janie. She was sort of cow culture royalty. Her family owned one of the biggest cattle ranches in Texas. Janie had spent a lot of time, as rich folks do, "making the scene" around the planet. You know the type, skiing in Aspen, the apartment in Paris, the French Riviera, anywhere the beautiful people congregate.

I was around for that wedding too. As an engagement gift to the future wife, Glenn hired Ray Charles to perform at the engagement party. It was supposed to be a big secret. Guess who was in charge of that and all the show's production details, including Ray Charles, his band, and the Raelettes... You got it!

Janie had traveled somewhere in Central or South America, where she met a tennis instructor named Frankie, soon to be called Frankie the Blade. She brought him back to the Aspen house and hired him initially as a tennis instructor to teach her how to play better and teach Glenn the basics of the rich and famous's primary sport.

Eventually, her marriage with Glenn fell apart. When Janie parted ways with Glenn, she left behind a lot of costly clothes. "Take all this stuff home to Toni," Glenn said. "I have no use for them." He was right. He had no use for them. I got it. They would just remind him of Janie and the unhappier portion of their marriage.

Toni took the clothes, and between Summer and Toni, they wore them out. Glenn also threw in a vibrator that had been Janie's. Toni thought it was a strange thing to gift someone, and it kind of creeped her out. I wasn't sure if he meant it as, "Here's something you can do while we're on the road," or what. Toni laughed and said, "I'm not using that thing. Icky! Hello…UNSANITARY!" Then she threw it in the trash.

Janie left, and Frankie stayed. Glenn wasn't that into tennis, but he kept Frankie on as caretaker of the Aspen house. Compared to the work we did on the road, Frankie had a cushy gig; watch the house, sign for an occasional package, meet the cable guy, the gas guy, whoever, show them in, and then go home when they were done. The most strenuous thing he ever did was sweep the snow off the roof of the house. That's it…tough gig! For that, he was rewarded with a small bungalow on the property where he lived rent-free.

In Aspen, Glenn bought an adjacent home owned by Jimmy Buffet to turn into a studio. The idea was to let Mike Harlow, his engineer, live there. There were plenty of rooms, and whatever artist he recorded would live there as well when they recorded there.

Frankie took exception to that. He was jealous of Mike. He considered himself king of the mountain, so to speak, and thought Mike a threat to his domain. Really there was no comparison. Mike Harlow was an experienced and accomplished and highly skilled recording engineer. Frankie, not having any experience or skills in the music business, had no clue what that meant. Glenn spent hours and days in the studio with Mike working side by side and crafting his tunes. Frankie had no idea the bond that forms between an artist and an engineer. A good engineer can be a crucial player in the process, the producer's right-hand man, and another member of the band, albeit one that plays the studio console and the effects. In the making of recorded music, he is the person that gets the sounds an artist hears only in his head.

Mike Harlow and I moved the entire studio from LA to Aspen. Frankie was recruited by Glenn to help us get it into the Buffet house and set it up. It may sound easy, but it was not. There was no street access, so we had to carry everything across dirt and uphill to get it into the studio.

It was no easy move. There were a lot of components to hand carry up the hill. To make matters worse, we had no wheels, no dollies, and no hand trucks. Nothing that could roll over the dirt.

The whole time, Mike and I were struggling, and Frankie was whining. I don't think he'd ever done any manual labor before in his life. On top of that, he and Mike Harlow were continually bickering. Frankie just wouldn't leave him be.

As the engineer, Mike knew the studio components and how to set them up and was sort of the boss of the move. I was OK with that, but Frankie hated Mike from the get-go and was not one to let it go. He was all over Mike all the time.

Frankie's animosity had come to a head, and it was petty.

Inevitably it erupted into a full-blown argument. Frankie was screaming at Mike, and Mike was trying to fend him off.

In the distance, I heard Mike shout, "Go ahead, cut me, cut me. You'll pay, cut me." I ran out to where they were facing off with each other. Frankie had a knife in his hand, threatening to cut Mike, swishing the blade back and forth in front of him at Mike. Mike was screaming, "go ahead and cut me, I'll tell Glenn, and you'll be finished."

The bottom line is that Frankie thought his access to Glenn's property made him the number one boy. In reality, there was no contest and no pecking order and no "boys." We were all just Glenn's guys, each with our areas of responsibility. Frankie was nothing but a glorified caretaker and a minor league gigolo whose only previous work experience was to keep a wealthy female client's company and work them out on the tennis court.

And that is how Frankie the lame became Frankie The Blade.

No one knew it then, but Mike's time on earth would soon end. He dropped dead from a heart attack a short time later in Glenn's LA recording studio.

Nice Catch Reward

Henley, Frey, Walsh

Glenn Frey, Don Henley 1980s

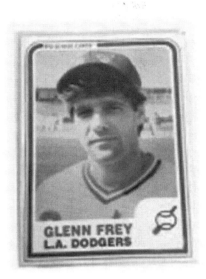

GLENN FREY
L.A. DODGERS

Dodgers Baseball Camp

B.J. THOMPSON
EAGLES-GLENN FREY

SPECIAL GUEST

BACKSTAGE
EUROPE 1988
FLEETWOOD MAC

THEATRE
BACKSTAG
EAGLES 5-18

3E
THIRD ENCORE

GUEST

Eagles

PLUS
JOHN DAVID SOUTHER

THE FORUM
1
PACIFIC PRESENTATIONS   AND CONCERTS WEST

Chicago

Working Personn

TURNER

PRIVATE
DANCER
TOUR
85

ACCESS
ALL AREAS

REO
SPEEDWAGON

GUEST

JACKSON BROWNE
TOUR 83

TOUR PERSONNEL
ALL ACCESS

11

Birds Of Prey

My era with the Eagles was the 1980s, which I consider the group's golden age. It was a well-known fact within the group that Glenn Frey and Don Henley *were* the group. They were the bosses. We all worked for them, and they didn't really rub our noses in it unless we screwed up. We were a team, dominoes in the chain of Eagles tour production. If we faltered, they faltered. None of us were irreplaceable.

We worked for craftsmen of the highest order, and we carried our weight at that level. As they did with their instruments, we were expected to execute our duties with focus, timing, and enthusiasm. Every note made a chord, every lick rode the beat. Everything fell nicely into place like a grandfather clock, each gear tooth falling in between teeth of the next wheel. A "groove" that ticked along like a Swiss watch and didn't miss a tick, a tock, a cue, or a minute of time.

Apart from the bosses, Joe Walsh was every crewmember's favorite Eagle. Don Felder was our least favorite. Timothy Schmidt kept a low profile, apart from asking me every night before the show, when she was there, to make sure his wife off in the wings got a cigarette, Timothy was almost the invisible man.

Joe Vitale, an occasional tour player, was a close friend of Walsh. The sorcerer's apprentice, Vitale, was almost as funny and "mischievous" as Walsh.

Joe Walsh was a big star in his own right before he joined the Eagles. Joe had no pretensions, nothing to prove, and no excess or sickness of ambition. He'd been there and done that, on his own. Joe was precisely who Joe wanted to be and was committed to playing his part in the Eagles' overall concept. His guitar spoke for him, and he sang in harmony with the other band members. Joe came to play.

Despite his reputation as a wild man, Joe had a huge heart. Sure, he had guitar technique, and he worked out his parts with Felder, but for the most part, when Joe stepped out and ripped off a lick, the universe flowed through him. Notes came from somewhere deep inside him, flowed out his fingers, danced across the strings onto the fretboard, through his amp and into the hearts and minds of the audience, and they loved him. Joe made love to the universe. It felt good to him, and it made everyone around him feel good too.

With little effort apart from just being himself, the universe rewarded him for revealing his heart, and he was self-deprecating. As Joe himself said, he had a mansion he'd never seen and forgot the price. A car that did one eighty-five, but he lost his license and couldn't drive. Yet he was thankful that life had been good to him.

I think of Joe as a larger than life lovable Spicoli, Sean Penn's character in the movie *Fast Times At Ridgemont High*. He was the likable stoner kid that in high school ordered a pizza delivered to class.

But Joe was way more than just a stoner. He was Spicoli with a heart and a soul that flowed out of his guitar. He was funny and lovable, disheveled and chaotic and tragic, yet heroic in his own element. When Joe's fingers touched the strings, magic happened. The cosmos poured forth in abundance. Joe was much more than Spicoli. He was Spicoli on Acid and Steroids, the clown prince of rock n roll and one of the most prolific sages of the instrument in his time. You can't not like Joe. Even when he's ripping down a hotel room wall with a chainsaw in the middle of the night. You'll cheer him on and want him to be your best friend, your brother. All inconsistencies considered; Joe will never let you down. He'll always be Joe. And you'll always love him for it.

Don Henley had a great drum tech named Tony Taibi, one of my closest friends. Of the two bosses, "The Gods," Henley was the most complex. Along with Glenn, the two of them had founded the group in the days after they were back-up musicians for Linda Ronstadt. He was multi-talented, a decent drummer, songwriter, singer, and an OK boss. Henley was known for the precision and attention to detail he brought to every aspect of the band, whether writing, recording, or the live touring shows we did.

In Don Felder's book, *Heaven And Hell,* he highlighted another aspect of Henley, his seriousness. He says no-one could "suck the fun out of a room" faster than Henley. Felder calls him "Grandpa." I'd heard the term, but I knew that Henley could be as much fun as any other band member and easily out prank Felder on his worst day. For the most part, Henley treated the crew with respect, whereas Felder complained to Irving that the band was paying for us "lackeys" to be on retainer when we were off the road. He said so in his book.

Since my first days with the band when I rescued him from stepping off the stage with the "nice catch," as it became known, I had earned Glenn Frey's trust and respect, and he always rewarded me for my efforts

Glenn was like that. He would reward you for a job well done or a show of loyalty. Above all, Glenn was a loyal guy and didn't hesitate to reciprocate. But if Glenn didn't like you or you screwed up something for him, he'd throw his favorite hockey term at you, and you'd be "off the ice" in the penalty box, and you'd have to earn your way back in. If he didn't like you or you somehow pissed him off, he'd say, "Just get away from me," or "Keep him away from me."

Glenn had a wicked sense of humor, and he messed with me always, another validation that we got on as friends and not just as his employee. Sometimes when I reached out of the shadows to hand him a guitar, he'd pull back a few steps, and I'd have to lean into the light. Then he'd step back farther, luring me to the front of the audience in the full luminance of the stage lights where the audience could see me. He knew I hated being in the spotlight, and he'd pull me farther and farther out into that world.

One night he had a problem with his pedalboard. He kept kicking at it with his shoe, but it only made it worse. He signaled me to come out and take a look at it when the lights were dim. I went out and had to get down on my hands and knees to get a closer look at it. I was on all fours when I figured out that a connector between two units had come out. I was working as fast as I could to get it fixed so I could get off the stage in compliance with the unwritten roadie creed: "be invisible, get it done, and never become part of the show."

Glenn talked to the audience about me as I worked, making up for the silence while fixing his gear. "This is Norton," he said. "He looks like a little pet down there, doesn't he? He's my pet."

Then he sat on my back. I was trying to work as fast as I could to get the hell out of there. He was enjoying himself at my expense. Finally, I got it done and headed back to my world in the shadows with him still chuckling to himself.

But Glenn would fight a lion for me or anyone he liked or loved. If anyone put me down in his presence, he'd be all over them for it. If I had a problem with some arrangement I was working on, he'd offer to "put his weight on it," meaning he'd speak to them himself because nobody refuses a celebrity. But I'd wave him off and let him know that I had it.

That was all out of loyalty and respect, and mischievousness. Glenn had all those qualities and more.

Jackson Brown gave Glenn his main guitar. It was a black Les Paul Junior. Glenn called it "Old Black." That guitar was a prized possession of Glenn's. I took care of it like it was a fragile little toddler. I even had to buy airplane seats for it from time to time, so it didn't have to go in the cargo hold.

One-night, Henley jumped off his drum riser, knocked Old Black over, and broke the headstock off. I called John Caruthers, owner of a well-known guitar shop in the San Fernando Valley, at about eleven o'clock in the evening to perform emergency surgery.

"John, I hate to do this to you, man, but I gotta meet you at the shop. Henley knocked Frey's main guitar over on stage and broke the headstock clean off. We're back on the road in two days. We have to have it by then."

John Caruthers had the best guitar shop in LA. Every rock star and every guitar player in LA knew of him and most likely had work done by him at one time or another. John did not disappoint me, he never did, and his work spoke for itself.

Glenn would occasionally call me before a tour to make a department store run for him. "Norton, I need you to make a run for me. I need two dozen pairs of underwear." Glenn wore underwear on the road only once, then he'd throw them away and put on a brand-new pair. He rarely ever shopped for himself for fear of being recognized, especially for underwear.

AWKWARD…!

My era with the Eagles was the 1980s, which I consider the group's golden age. It was a well-known fact within the group that Glenn Frey and Don Henley *were* the group. They were the bosses. We all worked for them, and they didn't really rub our noses in it unless we screwed up. We were a team, dominoes in the chain of Eagles tour production. If we faltered, they faltered. None of us were irreplaceable.

We worked for craftsmen of the highest order, and we carried our weight at that level. As they did with their instruments, we were expected to execute our duties with focus, timing, and enthusiasm. Every note made a chord, every lick rode the beat. Everything fell nicely into place like a grandfather clock, each gear tooth falling in between teeth of the next wheel. A "groove" that ticked along like a Swiss watch and didn't miss a tick, a tock, a cue, or a minute of time.

Apart from the bosses, Joe Walsh was every crewmember's favorite Eagle. Don Felder was our least favorite. Timothy

Schmidt kept a low profile, apart from asking me every night before the show, when she was there, to make sure his wife off in the wings got a cigarette, Timothy was almost the invisible man.

Joe Vitale, an occasional tour player, was a close friend of Walsh. The sorcerer's apprentice, Vitale, was almost as funny and "mischievous" as Walsh.

Joe Walsh was a big star in his own right before he joined the Eagles. Joe had no pretensions, nothing to prove, and no excess or sickness of ambition. He'd been there and done that, on his own. Joe was precisely who Joe wanted to be and was committed to playing his part in the Eagles' overall concept. His guitar spoke for him, and he sang in harmony with the other band members. Joe came to play.

Despite his reputation as a wild man, Joe had a huge heart. Sure, he had guitar technique, and he worked out his parts with Felder, but for the most part, when Joe stepped out and ripped off a lick, the universe flowed through him. Notes came from somewhere deep inside him, flowed out his fingers, danced across the strings onto the fretboard, through his amp and into the hearts and minds of the audience, and they loved him. Joe made love to the universe. It felt good to him, and it made everyone around him feel good too.

With little effort apart from just being himself, the universe rewarded him for revealing his heart, and he was self-deprecating. As Joe himself said, he had a mansion he'd never seen and forgot the price. A car that did one eighty-five, but he lost his license and couldn't drive. Yet he was thankful that life had been good to him.

I think of Joe as a larger than life lovable Spicoli, Sean Penn's character in the movie *Fast Times At Ridgemont High*. He was the likable stoner kid that in high school ordered a pizza delivered to class.

But Joe was way more than just a stoner. He was Spicoli with a heart and a soul that flowed out of his guitar. He was funny and lovable, disheveled and chaotic and tragic, yet heroic in his own element. When Joe's fingers touched the strings, magic happened. The cosmos poured forth in abundance. Joe was much more than Spicoli. He was Spicoli on Acid and Steroids, the clown prince of rock n roll and one of the most prolific sages of the instrument in his time. You can't not like Joe. Even when he's ripping down a hotel room wall with a chainsaw in the middle of the night. You'll cheer him on and want him to be your best friend, your brother. All inconsistencies considered; Joe will never let you down. He'll always be Joe. And you'll always love him for it.

Don Henley had a great drum tech named Tony Taibi, one of my closest friends. Of the two bosses, "The Gods," Henley was the most complex. Along with Glenn, the two of them had founded the group in the days after they were back-up musicians for Linda Ronstadt. He was multi-talented, a decent drummer, songwriter, singer, and an OK boss. Henley was known for the precision and attention to detail he brought to every aspect of the band, whether writing, recording, or the live touring shows we did.

In Don Felder's book, *Heaven And Hell,* he highlighted another aspect of Henley, his seriousness. He says no-one could "suck the fun out of a room" faster than Henley. Felder calls him "Grandpa." I'd heard the term, but I knew that Henley could be as much fun as any other band member and easily out prank Felder on his worst day. For the most part, Henley treated the crew with respect, whereas Felder complained to Irving that the band was paying for us "lackeys" to be on retainer when we were off the road. He said so in his book.

Since my first days with the band when I rescued him from stepping off the stage with the "nice catch," as it became known, I had earned Glenn Frey's trust and respect, and he always rewarded me for my efforts

Glenn was like that. He would reward you for a job well done or a show of loyalty. Above all, Glenn was a loyal guy and didn't hesitate to reciprocate. But if Glenn didn't like you or you screwed up something for him, he'd throw his favorite hockey term at you, and you'd be "off the ice" in the penalty box, and you'd have to earn your way back in. If he didn't like you or you somehow pissed him off, he'd say, "Just get away from me," or "Keep him away from me."

Glenn had a wicked sense of humor, and he messed with me always, another validation that we got on as friends and not just as his employee. Sometimes when I reached out of the shadows to hand him a guitar, he'd pull back a few steps, and I'd have to lean into the light. Then he'd step back farther, luring me to the front of the audience in the full luminance of the stage lights where the audience could see me. He knew I hated being in the spotlight, and he'd pull me farther and farther out into that world.

One night he had a problem with his pedalboard. He kept kicking at it with his shoe, but it only made it worse. He signaled me to come out and take a look at it when the lights were dim. I went out and had to get down on my hands and knees to get a closer look at it. I was on all fours when I figured out that a connector between two units had come out. I was working as fast as I could to get it fixed so I could get off the stage in compliance with the unwritten roadie creed: "be invisible, get it done, and never become part of the show."

Glenn talked to the audience about me as I worked, making up for the silence while fixing his gear. "This is Norton," he said. "He looks like a little pet down there, doesn't he? He's my pet."

Then he sat on my back. I was trying to work as fast as I could to get the hell out of there. He was enjoying himself at my expense. Finally, I got it done and headed back to my world in the shadows with him still chuckling to himself.

But Glenn would fight a lion for me or anyone he liked or loved. If anyone put me down in his presence, he'd be all over them for it. If I had a problem with some arrangement I was working on, he'd offer to "put his weight on it," meaning he'd speak to them himself because nobody refuses a celebrity. But I'd wave him off and let him know that I had it.

That was all out of loyalty and respect, and mischievousness. Glenn had all those qualities and more.

Jackson Brown gave Glenn his main guitar. It was a black Les Paul Junior. Glenn called it "Old Black." That guitar was a prized possession of Glenn's. I took care of it like it was a fragile little toddler. I even had to buy airplane seats for it from time to time, so it didn't have to go in the cargo hold.

One-night, Henley jumped off his drum riser, knocked Old Black over, and broke the headstock off. I called John Caruthers, owner of a well-known guitar shop in the San Fernando Valley, at about eleven o'clock in the evening to perform emergency surgery.

"John, I hate to do this to you, man, but I gotta meet you at the shop. Henley knocked Frey's main guitar over on stage and broke the headstock clean off. We're back on the road in two days. We have to have it by then."

John Caruthers had the best guitar shop in LA. Every rock star and every guitar player in LA knew of him and most likely had work done by him at one time or another. John did not disappoint me, he never did, and his work spoke for itself.

Glenn would occasionally have me make a department store run for him. "Norton, I need you to make a run for me. I need two dozen pairs of underwear." Glenn wore underwear on the road only once, then he'd throw them away and put on a brand-new pair. He rarely ever shopped for himself for fear of being recognized, especially for underwear. AWKWARD!

12

Road Warriors

Touring with the Eagles could be exciting, exhausting, exhilarating, bizarre, quirky, surreal, frustrating, and rewarding, and that was on a good day. Most days were far above average. But no matter how many hours we put in and how frustrating it got, we always enjoyed it.

Checking the group into a hotel was a nightmare. Thank God it was someone else's nightmare. The band all stayed on one floor and the crew on another. Every band member required a suite. Every hotel has a fixed number of suites, and new suites could not be manufactured on the spot to fill the band quota. The road managers had to find ways to get equal rooms for all the players. Don Felder even talks about it in his book, *Heaven and*

Hell. He talks about how he was not one to be slighted with a lesser room than the others. He patrolled the halls checking accommodations to make sure he got his due.

The band members frequently wound each other up about their rooms. Someone would claim to have a grand piano in the room or a sauna, or a fully stocked bar just to get a rise out of each other. I know of another band's crew that did something similar but to a lesser degree. When they boarded their transportation for the day, usually hungover from a night of Bushmills Irish Whiskey, someone would complain that the pool filter was dirty in their room, and someone else would say, "Yeah, I couldn't get the pinout of the cup on the third hole of my golf course." From there, the story grew to epic proportions, and everyone had a laugh.

It all started in the Eagles when Don Henley declared that he had a bad back, and he'd need a specific mattress on the road. It took a week to find the one that satisfied him. That opened the floodgates. Pretty soon, Felder was complaining of pain in his lower back when he played steel guitar. That caused *us* pain; in our asses!

We ended up carrying five mattresses on a dedicated mattress truck, one for each band member. The truck rolled up in the morning, and the show promoter had a crew (two to a mattress) waiting to carry them into the hotel, remove the hotel mattress and install each band member's mattress. Each one was specific to a band member and had the name of that person on its cover.

Anticipating that some promoters would balk at the idea ("Enough is enough already,") Eagles staff would say, "if there's a problem, let us know. I'm sure Irving would be happy to work it out with you." Not wanting a call from the Supreme Being and God of fire and fury, they would give in.

It amounted to a local crew of mattress loaders, provided by show promoters, to get them in the room. The road crew was already gone and on the way to the next city when it came time to take them out. Then there was a separate crew call for men to remove the mattresses and reload the mattress truck. Because of the logistics involved, there were some days when the mattress truck could not get to the next city in time. The buzz among the band at soundcheck was, "Are we getting mattresses tonight?"

Carrying the mattresses was the easy part. It just took several men, two to a mattress. Imagine booking forty or so rooms in a five-star hotel. When the booking was made, and the deal was done, an "Oh by the way" was added.

"Oh, and by the way, the Eagles will be supplying their own mattresses. You're gonna need to store the hotels five mattresses. A local crew will carry theirs in and up to the rooms. At check-out time, they'll be back to remove them. And uh …have a nice day!"

From the crew's perspective, the band members, all but Felder, were relatively easy to work with on stage. On my side of the stage, Glenn had me put a 7 oz Coca Cola with ice, a few extra guitar picks, a pack of Marlboros, and a lighter on top of his amp. Timothy Schmidt asked for nothing except a cigarette for his wife, and never in my time with the band did he ever ask me to change the strings on his bass.

Felder had requirements, but I had my hands full with Glenn and didn't pay much attention to him unless there was an emergency and his guy Jimmy Collins needed my help. Tony Taibi looked after Henley, who occasionally needed a new snare to cover for a broken head. He also kept him amply supplied with sticks.

The Joe Walsh of my era with the band, the 1980s, was another story. Much of the time, Joe showed up with minutes to spare. Joe was like a boxer slumped in his corner in the 8th round of a fight he was losing badly. Sometimes at showtime, I could sense when he made it to the stage. I'd see his cornermen, road manager Smokey, and Guitar tech Jage Jackson, scrambling to get their guy in the ring as he swayed back and forth in place. Jage would place the guitar strap over his neck, hand him a pick and point him to the stage. Sometimes Joe called out for a bandana, and Smokey pulled out a pile of bandana's and let Joe choose one. With his guitar and bandana firmly in place, Joe was ready, and the show could begin. I imagined Smokey holding up a pile of bandana's for Joe's approval, trying to color coordinate it with his "outfit," and Joe slurring, "No, give me the red one… I want the red one, man." Like it really made a difference. Joe usually went on stage in the same grubby outfit he wore for days at a time.

Joe made a couple of spectacular last-minute entrances to the venue, always arriving just in time to step out on to the stage. The best entrance I ever saw was classic Joe. He was running late; in fact, the show was held for him. He was half in the bag from whatever he'd partied on the night before, and there was no way they could get him to the venue through traffic. That would mean further delays and the embarrassment of facing his bandmates, especially Glenn and Don. The only way to get him through traffic was with lights and sirens…so they called him an ambulance. The driver cranked up the lights and sirens, and once again, Joe made it to the show in the nick of time.

One night after a show, Joe came to me for help on the down low. He was hungry and craving a ham and cheese sandwich. "I need a ham and cheese sandwich," he said. "I'll pay anything."

There was no way I could leave the venue to find him a sandwich, so I went to the in-house concessionaire and confided in him. "I need your help," I said. "Joe Walsh needs a ham and cheese sandwich, and you're my best bet to get that done. Can you help me out?" The guy looked at me like I was nuts. I said, "Listen, I can make it worth your while. What do you want?" I was thinking like 20 bucks. Then he called his boss. When he hung up, he looked me dead in the eye and said $75. I gave the sandwich to Joe and said, "I hope you enjoy it, I had to pay $75 for it, and the guy wouldn't budge on the price." Joe didn't care; $ 75 was nothing to him. But he did ask me not to let the other band members know. Joe wasn't worried about the money, but he knew they'd never let him hear the end of it if they found out.

I never ratted him out, but they found out anyway. He was right; he never heard the end of it.

There were some, honestly, *many* nights, when Joe was really wasted. His guys pushed him out on stage, and he'd play flawlessly, never missing a chord, or a note, or blowing it in any way. His playing was absolutely perfect and typically Joe Walsh, with the universe once again at the helm.

When the song ended, he had to change guitars. He'd sometimes just stop, locked in place, welded to the stage. Smokey and Jage called out to him from the far reaches of the universe behind the amp line, through time and space, "Joe, Joe…"

They were Joe's tether from our world to whatever dimension he occupied at the time. But Joe always played great, even though at times he wasn't in charge and his fingers channeled a higher power.

There were times at the end of a song when instead of changing guitars, he'd throw the current instrument towards Jage. Jage had a good average of spectacular catches.

We had great respect for all the individual band instruments and maintained them like they were toddlers. They were our children. Many had been customized specifically to the player's specifications.

When Joe sailed a guitar at you, you'd never know where it was headed. We were like the proverbial fire brigade running around with a net trying to catch a baby thrown from the window of a burning building. Sometimes it was caught, other times not.

We'd be up all night on the bus trying to put the pick-ups back in place and fix any other damages before the next show.

It got to the point where on the last song, Joe would randomly lob his guitar up in the air. No one ever knew where it was going to land. Me and Jimmy Collins would move clear over from our side of the stage to help Jage out. (No one wanted to be up all night with an impossible repair job on a priceless guitar.) I had a guitar stand in place for Glenn, so I didn't have to worry about his instrument, and Jimmy and I could run over to help Jage catch Joe's guitar.

Sometimes we'd run into Joe in the halls or the hotel lobby, and he'd say, let's go out somewhere. He didn't care, crew, band, truck, and bus drivers, whoever was around were invited. We'd end up in some local bar or beer joint, and it was Joe's party.

Some artists don't get the crew. They don't understand what we do or don't appreciate us, or flat out don't care. They consider guys like us just the help. They just want things done for them at their whims. Arrogance can be rampant in a rock n roll band. Others, like the Eagles, while they demanded our best, were not like that. They got it and appreciated the work we did. They showed it in many different ways, like the bonus I got for the "nice catch," the food and beverages they brought in for rehearsals, the decent hot meals in the contract rider, and the per diem and paychecks we received on time, every time. We felt appreciated by the band members, all but one that is.

Overall my time with the Eagles was a pleasure. We didn't sleep much, and we worked long, hard hours (fourteen to sixteen-hour days) harder than most people (*most*) work at their day jobs from nine to five. But it was truly a pleasure.

In their more collegial moments on tour, the band played a card game they called Eagle poker. Glenn Frey claimed he had invented the game in his early days in Detroit. The game is a derivative of an old game called Acey-Deucy or Red Dog. You bet on whether or not a third card's value will fall between the other two dealt cards.

When the band was in England recording with Glyn Johns, there was no drinking or drugs allowed in the studio. But he had no problem with gambling, so the band members engaged in the only vice available to them. They gambled for endless hours and perfected the game.

In the Early days, when the Eagles toured the UK with Neil Young, Henley was engaged in a feud with Neil's producer. He was continually razzing the band. Henley needed a way to get back at him and found a way to get his revenge. Henley challenged him to Eagle poker. The game was a marathon that went on for hours. When it was over, Henley had beaten him for $7,000.

Felder, in his book, *Heaven and Hell...*, talks about losing $1800 in a pot to a roadie. Imagine that, a mere roadie, one of the "bunch of lackeys," he complained to Irving about. It was such a blow to his ego that he quit playing after that.

But Eagle poker is an excellent example of what the two founders of the band, Frey and Henley, were made of. They were always willing to bet it all on their success. They hung in there to the end and wound up winning it all. They would never have cut and run after a losing streak.

The Eagles were known for the after-show party they threw in every city. We called it the Third Encore or 3E for short, and everyone knew it was Glenn and Don's party. It was an exclusive event, usually held in a suite in whatever hotel we were staying in. To qualify, you had to be over 18 and female, a band member, crew member, friend, or invited guest of the band.

Female guests and every loose woman in town were recruited from the audience, the local bar scene, or by referral of various local sources. Invited guests were issued a little pin-on button that simply read "3E."

During the show, one of the road managers supervised the set-up, which usually included a bathtub full of long neck Bud's on ice, Jack Daniels, and various other liquor choices.

Eagles security was posted at the elevators. They checked badges and, in some cases ID's and cleared non badged guests by way of walkie talkies. The party began after the show. If the crew was going to make it we'd have to pack our gear, get it loaded on the trucks, and hustle back to the hotel in time. Some nights we made it, and on others, we didn't. On some nights, we were back on the bus, headed for the next city.

One night at home, my phone rang. It was a guy who did not introduce himself. Instead, he said, "You Norton?"

"Yeah, my name's Bob Thompson, but they call me Norton. Who is this," I said?

"Bob Thompson, with the Eagles?" Still, no introduction. "I heard you've got a lot of stories."

"Stories about what," I said.

"About the Eagles," he answered.

"Yeah, Yeah, I work with the Eagles," I said. "Did you clear this with Glenn Frey and Don Henley? They don't like putting their laundry in the street."

He came back with, "It's no problem."

Stringing him along, I said, "How much are you paying?"

"What do you mean, how much am I paying? I got stories from other guys; they didn't ask me for money."

"I don't know who you got stories from," I said. "You better run with those stories because that's all you're going to get."

"Can't you tell me a story," he said, "one story?"

I said, "I can't tell you anything but, GOODBYE," and I hung up the phone.

Occasionally, fans showed up at the stage door, sometimes more than one, with a guitar or few guitars they wanted to sell. Always looking for a competitive edge on bandmates, Felder made sure he was the first one there. We all just assumed it was so he could have first dibs on any rare items some unaware local kid had for sale.

13

Road Dogs

It was a dark stormy night. Really!

When morning broke, the sky was still dark with storm clouds. It was a miserably damp and rainy day at the Florida stadium The Eagles were playing that night. It could not have rained any harder. Everything was either wet or muddy. Road cases wouldn't roll to the stage, and everything was beaded in rainwater. The whole show site was a puddle of mud.

The crew bus came to a stop as close to the stage as we could possibly get. We stepped off the bus into ankle-deep mud. The show promoter sensing our disgust, preemptively said, "I paid, the band plays."

Fortunately, the stage was covered. That did little to stop sheets of rain that blew on to the apron, the front of the stage nearest the audience, where most of the performance occurred. We reminded each other that practically everything on the stage was electric, and on a wet stage, electricity is not your friend.

Every road case left a trail of wheel tracks where they rolled across the stage, followed by a muddy shoe-print trail. But we toughed it out as we always did, and by soundcheck, we had the stage set and much of the mud onstage under control.

It rained all through the show, and as far as I know, not one fan left the sold-out venue until the show was over. When the last encore ended and the band left the stage, we tore down and packed up our gear. It never stopped raining. For the next few shows, we found dried-on and caked-up mud everywhere. It had been a fabulous few days in the glamorous backstage life of a roadie.

During a show, we had various cues that required us to be in a specific spot on the stage at a precise time, to either pass a guitar to our guy, or catch it while he scrambled to another instrument to make his cue in time. The Eagles were pretty good with that kind of stuff, and we had a sort of choreography worked out in advance. It was a dance, a well-timed move that allowed the player to join the song with the next instrument right on the beat, right on cue.

Other bands I'd worked with weren't always that well-coordinated. I had one guy in another big band that had to stop playing tambourine and pick up the next instrument at a crucial part in a song.

He'd throw me the tambourine offstage, and I'd catch it. But once we had the timing down, he'd mess with me. He'd throw it to the left or the right of me and get a kick out of watching me scramble for it. Sometimes I'd have to stretch like a first baseman with his foot on the bag and a fast runner barreling down the baseline.

A drummer I worked with a lot for a while was a great guy offstage and became a pain to work with onstage. He was going through a period where he broke drumheads all the time and getting angry and frustrated over it. The first time he threw a snare drum at me to change the head, I took it in stride. The second time I let it fall to the ground and pantomimed back at him, shrugging my shoulders, "Oops!" He never threw another drum.

There was a period on the road where we all indulged ourselves with white powder to keep our energy levels up. One of the tech crew was our supplier. He had an exclusive clientele, us. We told ourselves it was for purely medicinal purposes.

Each morning someone yelled, "Party line!" and we literally formed a line. We forked out whatever we could afford, usually our per diem. The wisest amongst us already had the office send our paychecks directly home, but we used our per diem in the party line.

One night after a long few days with little sleep, I decided I had time for a short nap that would revive me. After the hot dinner meal provided for us each night at the venue, I slipped away, looking for a quiet place to take a nap. The Back of Don Henley's drum riser onstage was open and looked inviting, a good place to catch a few winks undisturbed.

I thought no one would ever guess to look for me there.

I crawled in, and in an instant, I was in a deep sleep. I was finally getting a well-needed rest. Then in a half-dreaming -half-awake state, I became aware of a series of thumps coming from somewhere above me. I slowly came out of my coma and recognized a pattern and became aware that it was getting louder, "Boomp... Boomp boomp, Boomp... Boomp boomp, Boomp... Boomp boomp, Boomp... Boomp boomp. Still half asleep, I recognized it as the four-bar kick drum pattern Don Henley played to open the show.

I was startled, shocked, awake, and just barely aware of my situation. But I knew I was under the drum riser, and the show had begun without me. I could feel my long hair matted flat against the side of my face, held there by the spittle and drool that had leaked from me in sleep, something my crewmates and I called drool face and bus hair. I was a mess. I looked like an unmade bed.

My eyes were barely open, and I was still groggy. I managed to wriggle out of the riser and ran smack into Tony Taibi, Henley's drum tech. I was lucky to have crawled out on the backstage side of the riser. If I'd stumbled out on the front side, I would have been the show that night, and an unemployed roadie.

"Where do I go," I groaned in confusion.

Tony pointed to my spot and said, "Go! Over there!"

I army-crawled all the way over to the other side of the stage to my spot where I had a guitar change for Glenn.

When I reached out of the shadows to hand him the guitar, he moved back slightly toward the front of the stage. He was messing with me again, trying to drag me out into the light.

I whispered, "where you going..."

Glenn snapped back, "Where were you..."

I whispered, "I'll tell you later."

Glenn moved back a few steps more, "I said, where were you?"

"Glenn," I said, "please, not tonight, my grandmother's in the audience."

"Where is she," he answered.

"In the third row, over there," I pointed.

At that point, he dropped his guard, and I grabbed the guitar and switched it. For the next three songs, he kept asking me, "Where is she Norton, where is your Grandmother..."

My grandmother wasn't even in the state. He was on to me.

After the show, he asked to see me and then read me the riot act, all 100 chapters. He reamed me up one side and down the other. I had never been reamed like that by him before, or since.

The Eagles show had several set carts used to transport rolls of Marley floor covering and other items used on our stage set. A typical set cart consists of a metal framework about 8 feet by 3 feet on sturdy lockable casters. A 3 feet high A-frame has several crossbars with grooved slots across the ends on both the cart's short ends. The Marley rolls are placed lengthwise between the slots on both sides of the A-frame. Set carts are big and bulky, and they take up a lot of truck space. We always put them on the tail end of the truck because they had to be first to come off at each venue.

We loaded out of a venue and were on the bus headed for the next show. After the usual stop at a truck stop for gas and snacks and what-not, we were back on the bus heading down the highway. Suddenly a thought came crashing into my head. It hit me like a ton of bricks. It was a bad feeling so strong that I asked the bus driver to radio the truck and let him know that we were pulling over and needed to look inside his truck. We pulled over, popped the doors on the truck, and sure enough, no set carts! They'd been left at the venue, most likely on the loading dock.

I rang up the promoter and got no answer, just a machine spewing useless information. "No, no," I growled at myself into the phone. "I don't need a friggin machine; I need my Marley carts." Back on the bus, I announced," We're going back to the venue. If I have to break a window, we're getting those carts."

The truck and crew bus made the first U-turn and headed back to the venue. The venue building that earlier had been alive with Eagles fans' joy and adoration was now dark and scary and a big lump on the landscape, like the one in the pit of my stomach.

As we pulled into the venue, a light from the loading area was visible in the distance. It offered a small amount of hope. Then we drew nearer, and it became apparent the cleaning crew was still at work, and the carts were near the door.

I found the guy in charge and said, "I need to get into that loading bay and load those five carts. They were left behind." He balked at first. That is until I waved a hundred-dollar bill at him. We loaded the carts, and before long, we were back on the road, 50 miles out of our way, and behind schedule. But we were heading in the right direction.

My crewmates and the bus and truck drivers were pissed off at me because of the delay and uncertainty and stress of not knowing if we could retrieve the set carts. But we got lucky. We rescued them, moved on, and lived to fight another day.

The next day at the load in, when the truck doors opened, and all five carts were sitting there, everyone realized what a hassle it would have been without them, especially if any of the bosses found out. I ended up being a hero, after all.

On a touring crew's bus, certain etiquettes are rigidly enforced. One of the first things you learn when you're one of seven or eight guys and/or girls on a bus is never to show up late. Some bands have a grace period of 10 minutes, some less. If you miss the bus, you'll find what some bands call the "oil spot" or the "grease spot" waiting for you. That's the little puddle of oil the bus leaves behind on the pavement after it leaves without you. With the Eagles, we had a 15-minute late charge. If you exceeded the fifteen-minute grace period, the bus would go on without you, and you had to pay for the cab to the venue. One tour manager, Jim Cantale, left the band's big shot manager behind after numerous calls to the room and a knock on her door. The gig was about an hour away, and the cab fare was enormous. She was furious when she arrived, but the artists defended the rule.

Everyone that has toured and ridden on the crew bus knows there is a proper way to sleep in a bus bunk. Tony Taibi slept incorrectly.

The correct way to sleep in a bus bunk is with your feet to the driver. Tony slept with his head to the driver. He clearly did not know how to sleep on a bus. We had to teach him.

Toilet etiquette is essential. On the first day of any tour, I had a speech, "We do not shit in the toilet, and we don't pee in the aisle."

Pooping in the toilet will pollute the air on the bus for a long time. If you have to wake up to pee, remember, you are on a bus. Try to make it to the little room on the driver's side.

I used to sleep in what I call my bus uniform. I wore pajamas. When the production manager woke me in the morning to set the risers, I'd roll out of my bunk, put on my robe and slippers. I'd head into the venue to supervise the placement of band risers on the stage. I'd direct the local stagehands to do the heavy lifting, and when the job was done, I'd slip quietly back into my bunk for a few hours while the sound and lighting technicians did their thing. Later in the day, when they were done, I'd go back in, take a shower, continue with my set-up of Glenn's gear, and then tune more than ten of Glenn's guitars and spares. (Every guitar had a spare.)

Another point of etiquette on the bus is to quietly close the doors to the sleeping compartment, and when you exit the bus, walk slowly down the steps, don't run. Running could rock the bus and wake up the light sleepers. You do not want to wake up a roadie that finally got to sleep after a long day of load-in, a show, and a long load out. You will suffer his or her wrath and fury.

One morning, I woke up to do what I do and was almost entirely out of my bunk when my bare foot landed on a strange feeling texture. It was a bizarre sensation. Then I realized I had landed on a human head. It was the head of one of my crewmates that had been inebriated in one way or another the previous night and never made it into his bunk. The only thing that saved me from coming down hard on his entire body was the little hop-step I did with the initial sensation. Fortunately, he was OK, still anesthetized, and oblivious to his surroundings. I was the one who was shaken up. It is bizarre to wake up in the morning on a tour bus and step on a human head. Very bizarre!

I used to sleep in the middle bunk in the back, on the left. One typical night I crawled into the rack anticipating a solid night's rest en route to our next gig. I awoke a short time later to a strange smell, a combination of burning rubber and smoke.

I remembered feeling a big bump in my sleep that must have been what woke me up. Then I saw smoke, real smoke, not dream smoke, pouring out from the bunk below me. I jumped out of bed and saw the bus's smoking rear tire in the space where the bunk below me had been. Fortunately, no one had been assigned that bunk.

The bus came to an abrupt halt on the side of the road. In full abandon ship mode, I shouted for everyone to get off the bus.

There was no panic, just a flurry of half-awake roadies grabbing their hand luggage and making a hasty exit for the door. We were lucky, very lucky. There were no casualties and no injuries, but I had never been so scared in my life.

Cops came to the accident scene to make a report. There were a lot of ooh's and ahs amongst them. "That was a close one," they all said. "I've never seen that before." If a highway cop hasn't seen something before, you know it's terrible.

"You don't have to remind me," I said. "I know how close it was." When confronted, the driver couldn't remember anything, at least that was his story. Best guess was that he had either fallen asleep and jumped a curb, or just plain hit a curb or some other obstruction in the highway. He stuck to his story and most likely saved his license. We never did learn what had actually happened. We were all just thankful to be alive. But we had no time to try and figure it out; we still had hours and miles to go before we got to the venue.

We had a load-in, and a soundcheck to do the next day and a show to do that night, beginning a few hours later. I cornered the driver, himself in a bit of shock, and laid out the situation. We needed another bus, and we needed it now. Somehow, he was able to pull that together, and a standard greyhound type bus, what I call a sit up bus, arrived later. "There was no more laying down that night."

We had things on our bus that we had to transfer to the sit-up bus. Our workday had already begun in the middle of the night. Given the new bus's rigid seating arrangements, there was not much solid sleep to be had that night. But as always, we made it to the gig and got the job done.

Then the audience arrived, just another show in another town. The fans saw a great show and heard their favorite songs and left with smiles on their faces, completely unaware of what a band crew goes through at times to make a show happen.

For a time, the stage crew flew on commercial flights to all our gigs. Some nights when we were able to make it to the 3E party, we left in the wee hours with an early morning flight to catch. Our logic was: why even get into a bed you can only be in for an hour or two. It made no sense to us. We'd go right to the airport, check-in, go directly to the gate, find a quiet corner on the floor near the gate, and spread out to sleep for as long as we could. Often a gate agent woke us up when they announced the flight. We'd march down the jetway like Zombie survivors of the night of the living dead.

Our seats were usually blocked together near the back of the plane. We called our section the Joey Dolan lounge after an old washed-up fighter Named Joe Dolan, dubbed "*The Irish Dead-End Kid.*" And that's what we were too. We were the Dead-End Kids of rock n roll. Young and energetic, indestructible, and bulletproof, we leaped tall buildings in a single bound. Sleep - what's that...? Sleep didn't tell *us* what to do; we told sleep when it was time to rest.

Many Eagle fans came partly to see the guitars. Between all the band members, we had a total of about 40 guitars. We stanchioned them off before the show and allowed people to come up to the stage and gawk at them like cars on display at a car show or a diorama in a museum. Then they'd take their seats and hoot and holler and have a good time and enjoy the show.
What most people don't realize is that every show begins as a construction project. We arrived to load in a show in an empty room: just four walls, seats, a floor, and a ceiling. Local stagehands erected a stage, and we placed band risers on top of it than surrounded it with instruments and amplifiers. But before that happened, riggers climbed anywhere from 30 feet to 60 feet up into the rafters and attached lines and chain motors to hang sound and lighting and staging equipment. All in all, several tons of lighting, sound, and staging equipment ended up suspended from the ceiling.
JV was one of our lighting crew. One night in the middle of the show, I happened to notice a lamp had come loose from the lighting truss and was hanging right over Glenn's position on stage. I called it to JV's attention. There was only one way he could get to the lamp to fix it. He'd have to climb up to the truss and walk over to where the light was hanging, lay flat on the truss, and then reach down, pull it up, and secure it to the truss.

There was only one way up, which was by truss ladder, the aluminum equivalent of an old rope ladder. JV was the smallest, lightest guy on the crew, perfect for the job. I watched him slowly and deliberately climb the ladder, a tricky feat that had to be done cautiously so as not to shake the truss and cause movement in the lighting patterns on the stage. I watched him climb the 40 feet up to the truss in the middle of a show. He inched his way across the truss to get to the lamp, then secured it and inched his way slowly back and down the ladder. Not many people would have attempted that in the middle of a show with 15,000 people in the audience.

Sometimes celebrity entertainers "rewarded" their minions by taking them on the road. They'd say to me, "I want you to find something for my son or my kid brother, or my nephew, golf pro, tennis instructor, etc. etc. to do."

For a time, Glenn "gifted" me with his brother, studio engineer Mike Harlow, and his ex-wife's tennis instructor and Aspen caretaker, Frankie The Blade.

Mike could be useful, and though he'd never been on the road before, he at least had a clue. He had some knowledge of electronics and was overall a pretty smart guy and a talented studio engineer.

Glenn's brother could be pushed or berated into doing useful things, but you had to stay on him and watch him always, twenty-four seven. He thought he was entitled by bloodlines to a share in the "glamorous" world of rock n roll. But Glenn wanted him to earn his keep. He'd had an easy life at home for too long. He thought he was going to waltz into some cushy job as a guitar pick handler or something. Glenn was actually looking out for the kid, trying to "make a man out of him," so to speak.

Frankie the Blade, forget about it, was a prissy little wannabe gigolo that had made his living for years glomming on to the celebrity lifestyle in exchange for his services as a tennis or skiing instructor. He was no more suited to work on stage than I was to teach tennis.

Around the stage Frankie the Blade was even less help. The simplest tasks eluded him. Mostly what he did all day long was needle and wind up mike Harlow. Frankie was jealous of Mike's close relationship with Glenn in the studio and continuously tried to show that he was the better man.

My thoughts about it? As much as I liked Mike Harlow, all three of those guys were just taking up space on the bus. None of them had ever done a physical day's work in their lives. Being away from home was a terrible inconvenience to them, and they never stopped whining the whole time they were with us.

First day out, I gave Glenn's brother the lowest job on the tour, cleaning the Marley floor with acetone, just to see what he was made of. He failed at it miserably. Then he announced that he was going to ride on the band bus with the band. NOT! I reminded him what he was there for and put an end to that quickly. Besides, the band didn't want a newbie "civilian" on their bus either, Glenn's brother or not.

Overall the three of them combined couldn't make one decent roadie. All three were collectively less than useless.

If you want to be a roadie, you'd better be hearty, loyal, have a great attitude, and a love of music. Over and over again, when they whined, I repeated, "You wanted to come on the road. You're on the road!"

When The Eagles went overseas, they took all their own equipment. That meant loading everything into sea containers that would be transported by cargo ship. It could take weeks to get there.

In preparation, we had to compile an inventory of every piece of gear, it's country of manufacture, and a serial number. Then a carnet bond would have to be purchased. A carnet bond is a sort of passport for goods. It allows them permission to be transported in and out of any country that is a signatory to the international carnet agreement. This allows the goods to be temporarily imported into a country without being subjected to customs duty. It is a hall pass that allows you to go from one classroom to another without being detained by the hall monitors and sent to the principal's office.

In the early days' roadies did all the legwork on that. Now there are rock n roll companies that do it all for you. They send you an empty container, you load it, and they get you the carnet, ship it from the US, and deliver it to the venue in whatever city or cities in whatever country you're in. You just have to provide them with an inventory.

Clearing customs is another story. A customs inspector will often show up where the container is dropped to "inspect" the load. They are not always nice guys.

In Europe, we had customs inspectors show up and want to inspect each piece of gear to look for contraband, like drugs. German inspectors are exceptionally "thorough," and militant, and have a presumption of guilt right from the get-go.

They have required us to take the backs off amplifiers and speaker cabinets to do a "thorough" search. Not fun at all, especially when they're jabbering away at you in a language you don't speak or in a version of English you can't understand. Typically, three and a half hours later, well into our load-in time, they're still searching. That's the so-called "glamor" of rock n roll. Like I've said, it ain't easy being us; if it were, everyone would do it.

On one tour, we played the same venue for two days. The trucks and busses were allowed to park in the loading area for the run of the show. The two truck drivers and one of the bus drivers that happened to be the bus company owner's son were sitting in Glenn's bus playing video golf on the bus TV. While they played, they passed around a mason jar of Ever clear moonshine, another name for homemade hillbilly liquor. One problem, the bus company owners' kid didn't drink. This was his first foray into the evils of alcohol. "He didn't drink, smoke, or do anything, so he got really messed up."

To top it off, this was his first gig in rock n roll. "The Kid was brand new, still had a shine on him. It was amazing how twisted he got with so little in such a short time." He was so messed up that he locked himself in the bathroom, on Glenn's bus.

The truck driver came looking for me to tell me the kid was locked in the bathroom and ripped out of his mind. "How are you gonna get him out of there," they said.

"I don't know, but he's gotta be out of there before Glenn gets here, which is not too long from now, or it's my ass."

We ended up breaking the door down. We took the kid out and put him in one of our rental cars that were shuttling back and forth to the hotel.

"We gotta get this door fixed quickly," I said. "Glenn cannot see his bathroom door just hanging there."

I got a couple of the local stagehands and pleaded with them. "You guys gotta bail me out of this one. I'm stuck. Please, get this door fixed, like right now."

The stagehands pulled it off with time to spare before Glenn arrived, and I gave them a little something for their trouble.

That night, a sober version of the kid showed up. He was immediately pounced on by everyone he came in contact with.

"Wanna drink, young man?"

"Hey kid, wanna play some golf?"

"Need something to drink?"

"Better behave yourself from here on in…

"Don't make us tell your dad."

It had been a lesson the kid would not soon forget. Especially the fact that everyone on the tour gave him crap for it.

Hey kid, welcome to rock n roll.

14

Pranksters

It usually began with a phone call around 3am, and a disembodied voice floating across the wire from the other end, "I need my chain saw, man."

You've probably always wondered what it's like to hear a chainsaw starting up at 3am on a quiet floor in a 5-star hotel.

No? Really!

Not many people have. But when Joe Walsh played the chainsaw, they found out. Doors popped open up, and down the hallway, heads and torsos leaned out half asleep, wondering, "what the hell…"

Eagles tour personnel promptly appeared and passed among them, handing out hundred-dollar bills to get them back in their rooms.

"Sorry for the disturbance… Go Back to sleep."

"Here you go, Joe wants to buy you breakfast."

(Nothing to see here folks... yada-yada-yada!)

In Don Felder's book, he Says Irving bought Joe an electric chainsaw so he could keep the noise down. I never saw that one, "I was there for the noisy one. We got kicked out of a lot of hotels."

Joe once broke into a tour mate's room and painted the windows black. When the guy woke up, he thought it was still dark and went back to sleep. Stories about Joe's escapades were legendary, some witnessed, and some not. But if you knew Joe, odds are the wildest stories were the truest.

He shortened the legs on all the furniture in Irving's suite to "match" his diminutive stature. Another story talks about band members enlisting the supreme being to participate in trashes. Allegedly they got him to knock on someone's door and then step aside. Once he was identified through the peephole, the door would open, and other band members lying in wait doused the person with a water bucket.

In another favorite of Joe's, he glued a phone receiver to the unit. He'd ring the lucky person at four in the morning knowing they couldn't make it stop ringing without ripping the cord out of the wall.

Trashing rental cars was an old band trash used by Joe and many others as well. I've known bands to play bumper cars with rental vehicles. The Mac Davis band once did a two-state chase through Georgia and Tennessee, with two rental cars ambushing each other along the way with firecrackers and water balloons. The second car pulled into a small town in Georgia, stalking the first. Suddenly as they passed a used car lot, the first car pulled out of the display line and ambushed them with water balloons. Boys will be boys on the road.

There were always pranks between the band members, pranks and pranks, and rumors of pranks among the Eagles. Water balloons and water fights were standard. But there were numerous others, more elaborate and diabolical.

I was no stranger to pranks and trashes from as far back as I could go as a roadie. One closing night in Las Vegas with the Bellamy Brothers, I went out on stage during their big hit and filled Howard Bellamy's cowboy boot with shaving cream...with him in it.

Another prank I'd seen done in the early days was repeated with the Eagles. Two band members have differences. One takes a hot glue gun and glues the other's hotel room door shut. Eventually, hotel maintenance is called. They have to disassemble the door to get it open, which may or may not require a whole new door frame assembly that ends up costing that individual dearly.

One major league prank suitable for the prankster's hall of fame was perpetrated by an Eagles band member. Another band member had been incredibly annoying and obnoxious in his antics against his bandmate. The two were already locked in an ongoing feud, and band member #1 had had enough of ＿＿＿.

The prankster placed his own feces in a bag and snuck into his opponents' room. Unscrewing the grill from the heater vent, he put it in the ductwork and replaced the grill.

Later that night, the opponent returned to his room with a woman. When the woman left a moment later, she blamed the room's odor on his poor grooming habits. The "opponent" was clearly out of his league, an amateur when it came to band pranks.

I was backstage at another hit artists show with a female blues guitarist I worked with for a while before working with the Eagles. The other band kept calling her out onstage to jam with them, and she kept refusing because her guitar was locked in the truck.

Giving in to the invitation, she asked another crew member and me if we wouldn't mind getting her ax out of the truck.

"It's deep in the front of the semi, we said."

"I really want to jam with these guys," she pleaded.

"Oh, man," we said, we'd have to crawl the length of the semi-trailer to get to it.

"If you get my ax, I'll give you both a blowjob," she pleaded. "I mean it, I'll give you both head."

We knew her to be a lot of fun, crazy as a loon, and as nutty as a fruitcake. Neither of us was born yesterday, but we headed out to the truck.

We returned a short time later, hot and sweaty after crawling the length of the truck, all 42 feet, across the load, from the rear door to the nose. We slung cases aside, skinned our knees, and bruised our elbows to get to the artist's guitar trunk.

When we handed her the ax, she responded with, "Thanks, I owe you both a blowjob. GOTCHA!"

Another artist I worked with in the early days, Yvonne Elliman, enjoyed messing with me, in a humorous way. We were playing a cavernous old theater somewhere here in the US. Just before showtime, I got the band and singers in place on stage to start the show. When I went to Yvonne's dressing room to get her, she was gone. The band, antsy with pre-show nerves, were all over me. "Where is she? Where is she?"

I searched everywhere around the stage for her and couldn't find her anywhere. The clock had already ticked down to showtime, and she was nowhere to be found.

I spotted an old spiral staircase in a dark corner of the stage and climbed it to the top, thinking she may have wandered up there out of curiosity.

The space was dark and spooky, something out of Phantom Of The Opera.

I shouted, "Where are you? Let's go. It's showtime."

Off in the distance came a muffled reply from a mysterious little character voice.

"I'm over, he ee eer…"

"Where?" I replied. "I don't see you…"

From another part of the space, the little voice called out, "Over he ee er, come find me Nor or ton… come find me!"

She led me on a merry chase for a few minutes calling out in the little voice. Then she emerged from the shadows giggling. "Let's go, we have a show to do."

She was a great lady. She took us all with her to her home state of Hawaii at her expense. She loved Toni and insisted that she come along even though Toni was eight months pregnant with our daughter.

We enjoyed all that Hawaii had to offer; the mountains and the beaches where we swam, even Toni. A traditional Luau was put together for us by her parents. It had the traditional charcoal pit and a pig roasting over the coals. She was the nicest artist I've ever worked with.

On the Eagles tour, Carol Reed was the wardrobe person. She once made 20 black capes, one for each of the crew. We called ourselves the Monstertones and took a picture in front of the Marquee of the venue, which we changed to Read:

July 27, 28,29 SOLD OUT AN EVENING WITH
THE MONSTERTONES
(also) THE EAGLES

15

Roadie Wife

My name is Toni Thompson. "Norton" is my husband of 45 years, and I'm a roadie wife. I'm also the mother of a beautiful daughter, and I've survived cancer twice.

So, ladies, you wanna be a roadie wife?

Maybe you're already a roadie wife. Want to live a life of backstage glamour and privilege? Hang with the road crew? Get your own laminated backstage pass on a lanyard and the combination to the crew bus? You might even get to see all the band's shows from the wings while basking in the glory of rock n roll.

Perhaps one of the headliners will nod at you on his way to the stage. Maybe he'll invite you and your partner to his wedding. Maybe the lead singer's girlfriend will stand near you in the wings and wave to you as she leaves the venue in his limousine.

When your partner gets that dream tour, remember the party is out there in front of the barricade, the work, and it is work, hard work, is backstage behind the barrier. In the final analysis, you and your significant other, and the rest of the crew are the help. If you don't believe me check your bank account. Have a life, don't fall in love with someone else's lifestyle and pretend it's your own. Know it will someday end abruptly, sooner rather than later, because it will. Enjoy it while you can, because one day it will hit you. Touring with a show is a hard life. It is not for the weak or the faint of heart.

My marriage has survived several generations with hit bands and their road crews, including the Eagles, in their most significant era, the 1980s. We did OK by that while raising a daughter that now teaches eighth grade for a living.

We met in the 1960s when we were both a couple of "hippies" living in Hollywood, trying to find ourselves. A couple of girlfriends and me had come out to the West coast from South Bend, Indiana, where I grew up. I worked at Notre Dame University and had a second job to pay for the New Volkswagen my parents had bought me.

Four girlfriends and I worked together at an insurance company. One of our girlfriends got pregnant and moved to California so her parents wouldn't find out. One afternoon we said, "Let's get the hell out of here. Let's go to LA." Saturday morning, we all got on a plane with about a hundred dollars each to our names. In LA, we found a place on Barendo and Third Street.

Later my girlfriends and I moved into a big house in the Hollywood Hills that once belonged to Jimi Hendrix. It was an old Spanish style place with many arches, but it was a real mess.

Bobby was a charmer even then. He made his first pass at me by trying to heal the God-awful cold I had by filling me full of over the counter medications. Bobby made his move when I moved-in to another house where I was living with my girlfriends. I told him he could sleep with me if he kept his pants on. He kept his pants on until I discovered that he was a good guy and that I liked him.

In the beginning, Bobby did almost anything to make a buck for us. I worked as well. For a time, I worked at Capital Records, mainly as a switchboard operator. When calls came into Capitol from their artists, I routed them to the right person. Consequently, I spoke to many big celebrities on the label and, at times, helped them locate the person they called when they were out. Al Coury was Vice President of marketing and sales then. I worked closely with him at times. He was legendary for the work he did in developing artists like The Beatles, The Beach Boys,

Linda Ronstadt, Cher, and countless others. For a while, at Capitol, we had the Beatles downstairs in the recording studio. I got to meet everybody. Oddly, I wasn't that impressed with celebrity.

I worked for a time for an optometrist in Hollywood. Lionel Ritchie and the Commodores, as well as Hollywood moguls and film producers, came in to get their cool sunglasses. Then I landed a job working for a veterinarian. By then, Glenn Frey was part of our lives. I loved that job. I love animals.

One of the first groups Bobby ever worked for was Loggins and Messina. It was a short-term gig. I was brand new to the rock n roll world when I went to Loggins and Messina's show. "I was so fresh in that world that I was the one hiding in corners." Jimmy Messina was very, very nice. He came up to me and said, "You Have a beautiful haircut, and it looks so pretty on your face." He might have been hitting on me, but I don't think so. I didn't see it that way at all. I thought he was just a really nice guy. Besides, I didn't know I was exactly gorgeous, just a reasonably good-looking person. I think I only went to two Loggins and Messina shows.

Bobby was starting to go on the road a lot. Those early days are a lot of mumble jumble in my mind. But the one thing that sticks out really clearly in my head is, "I could never understand how Bobby could pack up his bags and just walk out of the house and leave me behind and leave me when I was pregnant."

Bobby worked with several one-hit artists in those early days. When he was with a one-hit band, all the women bonded. We'd go out to dinner, spend the night, do stupid things with make-up, and have a couple of beers. Once you get up into the more successful bands' ranks, it becomes more like a 24/7 business rather than like having the men off on a fishing trip or a golf outing.

The more successful bands and their wives live behind a celebrity wall and tend to gather with their own. Success brings a higher status. At that stage, many begin to relate to a level of society where they swore in their salad days they'd never belong. Many from humble beginnings end up members in good standing of the very hierarchy their art rebelled against. Often, they are seen flaunting their new-found status at high-end country clubs and charity affairs. I guess in many cases, if you've got it, you're obligated to flaunt it.

Bobby toured for a time with an artist named Walter Egan. A one-hit artist, his big hit called Magnet and Steel reached #8 on the Billboard Hot 100. Walter had a great band, and most of the players had wives. We all got along well and were a happy family. The band was traveling in an RV when I was pregnant with our daughter Summer. Occasionally I'd go to one of Walter's shows. I learned how to set up drums and guitars and everything else on the stage.

Bobby's biggest problem on the road with Walter was getting the female singer to show up on time. But she was a sweetheart, a bit wild but a sweetheart. We lived in a place with a pool in those days, and the girl would come by to hang out and swim. She was the only one that swam naked.

We were still innocent back then and really didn't have too much to commiserate about amongst the wives. For us to party back then was a matter of a couple of beers.

I was home alone one night while Bobby was on the road with Walter in San Francisco. It was about ten or eleven o'clock in the evening when I got a knock on the front door. I was living at home alone while Bobby was gone, and I was kind of leery of door knocks at that time of night. When I cautiously answered the door, there stood Bobby and the road manager, Steve. Bobby had two eyecups patched over his eyes.

I got him in the house and said, "What in the world happened to you?" He explained that he was tearing down the gear at the end of a show when someone threw a heavy three-pronged AC cord across the stage. There had been no horseplay and no malicious intent whatsoever, but it hit bobby in the eyes. It was merely an accident.

Bobby was taken to the hospital right away. Doctors said because his eye had filled with blood, he would need surgery. Walter hired a private jet to fly him home that night.

Kaiser Hospital in Northridge admitted him immediately and kept him for a few weeks. He had three surgeries and developed glaucoma. Blood kept on filling up in his eye, and the pressure got up to about fifty-six. Normal pressure was about eighteen.

Doctors said they had to patch both eyes because if you only patch one eye, the brain still uses both eyes. He was laid up for three weeks, and I stayed with him most of the time. We were afraid he would lose his sight. But he had another big fear while he was sightless. He was worried the hospital would catch fire, and he would not be able to get out. And, he hated hospital food.

One day the girl singer from Walter's band went by to see him. Bobby told me she ran her hand near his privates to know if he was still alive. He didn't feel a thing.

It was a rough time. Bobby was laid up and couldn't work, and I was pregnant and had toxemia and cancer, and I couldn't work either.

While Bobby was laid up, a good friend and guitar player with The Bellamy Brothers, John Beland, came by and gave us $100 to help us get by. "At that time, we had a dog, a Labrador named Pope. If Pope didn't like you, you didn't get into the house. He hated John. John had to take a screen off the kitchen window and slide an envelope into the house so that Pope wouldn't get him."

John also bought Bobby a two-way radio for Christmas so they could stay in touch. They each had a radio and a call sign.

John married a New Orleans girl named Mary, and we became close friends. Mary was a hoot. She was pretty, funny, and brilliant, and we had a blast together. She kept us girls in stitches with her antics, especially her gator impressions. When they had a little girl, they called her Sarah. Sarah eventually became part of our clique as well.

At Christmas, John asked Bobby to dress up as Santa Claus and visit Sarah at their home. Bobby went out and rented a costume and had Sarah sit on Santa's knee. He went through the usual "Ho-Ho-Ho spiel, "what do you want for Christmas, little girl?" Sarah tugged at his beard and said, "You're not Santa, you're Norton."

I found out I had cancer accidentally by getting my pregnancy exam. The doctor did the tests, and everything initially seemed to be OK. One day, when I worked for an optometrist on Hollywood Boulevard, Dr. Garrison, the phone rang. It was my MD calling to tell me I had cancer. He literally told me over the phone. Bobby was on the road, and I was by myself. This insensitive doctor from Kaiser Hospital tells me over the phone that I had cancer. "It was pretty scary."

To add to my fear, he explained that if he were to go in to test me, to find out how severe the cancer was, I would lose the baby.

Walter Egan kept Bobby on salary during his recovery, which enabled him to get disability, and that helped us out a lot.

I learned quickly as a roadie wife, gigs don't usually last forever, and it wasn't long before the Walter Egan gig ended. Sadly, we'd run into Walter Egan again, years later, when we moved to Nashville, but I'll let Bobby tell that story in a later chapter.

I was 7 months pregnant when Norton worked for Yvonne Elliman. "She was a sweetheart, a really nice lady." She was gracious enough to take us and the band and their wives to her family home in Hawaii. Yvonne's family threw us a big Luau with Hawaiian dancing and flowers and the whole bit. Bobby and I rented a car and went tripping around the island. One day Yvonne even flew us all to Maui.

I decided to go swimming in the ocean at 7 months pregnant, skimming across the water on my belly, and ended up in the hospital. You could walk out a half-mile in waist-deep water there, so I walked out to a float.

A big wave came in, and somehow, I lost the float. I had to

belly it all the way to the shore. Everyone was worried that I was going to lose the baby because I was hospitalized with toxemia. But It all worked out, and our daughter, Summer, was eventually born a normal kid.

Whenever I went out on the road, I would always pitch in. I can really coil-up some cable! Roadies that have seen my work always say, "I'll take her on the road anytime." I don't sit well. If I'm out there, I will make myself useful and not just sit on a road case like an idiot like some other women do when waiting for the guys to get done. Later I got the nickname "Soul Sister #1" from Glenn Frey.

Bobby was on the road with REO Speedwagon when they opened for the Eagles. The Eagles crew fell in love with him and found a job for him on tour. As it turned out, Glenn Frey liked him as well, and he became Glenn Frey's stage tech.

A short time before the Eagles had fully committed to hiring him, he again toured with REO. But the Eagles eventually committed, and he was officially hired on to work for Glenn.

The Eagles were a "boys club." They were all about "the guys." But I was probably the wife that had the most acceptance. No one other than the band and the working crew was allowed backstage. They kept it all very private. I knew there could be a lot of turmoil back there at times, and it was a controlled environment. They didn't allow anyone to see the turbulence. But I got a badge, and always the best seat in the house.

Glenn was very warm towards me. I got to know him, not so much with the others. Henley didn't seem like a bad guy, but I thought he kept himself in a glasshouse. You could see him, but you couldn't get too close.

I know for a fact that Glenn was very close to his mother. Every Sunday, he made a point of calling her, and every Christmas, he bought her a new Cadillac. He even bought her a place to live in Florida and eventually a home in Palm Springs.

On Glenn's fiftieth birthday, Bobby and I flew to Palm Springs for Glenn's birthday party at the elegant LaQuinta hotel. Glenn was always good to both Bobby and me. He was very kind to me, very respectful, and still under control.

Glenn and his partner Don Henley (The Eagles), were different people. Henley was a bit distant and protected himself at all times; Glenn could be open, generous, reachable, and very vulnerable much of the time. Yet he was a streetwise kid from Detroit. Because of that, he was a pretty good judge of character.

I grew up in South Bend, Indiana, and listened to WLS in Chicago, as did Glenn from his home in Detroit. Glenn and I had similar tastes in music. Whenever I was around him, we'd shout out song titles to each other, or names of recording artists from our hometown days.

Glenn was a sweetheart, always involved. Whenever he went out of town on his own, we shopped for him. I'd pick out the flowers Glenn liked to have in the house. He also had a housekeeper and a cook. His Cook was very kind to me. She taught me recipes and turned me on to the California Heritage Cookbook, and I still use it today.

When Bobby worked with the band, they were on the road most of the time, and every Christmas, we got a fat bonus check. When I went into the hospital for my hysterectomy, I got a huge bouquet of flowers from the Eagles. Everyone in the hospital thought I was really cool because I knew the Eagles.

On a video shoot, Glenn gave me my nickname "Soul Sister #1". He did his work and left, and it was time to break down the gear. About an hour later, Glenn walked back in. I was vacuuming the studio, and he asked me what I was doing, as if to say, you shouldn't have to clean up the studio.

He had a little blow and laid out some lines. I was not one to do a lot of blow. If I did one line, I'd be up all night ironing. Bobby could do a line and go right to sleep.

Blow is a yoyo. One hit gets you high for a short time, then you crash, and you need another line to get you back up. Someone once told me, "you can't just do one line. You either have to keep hitting it or quit and go to bed." You can't keep the yoyo going up and down, so you might as well go to sleep.

Bobby and I always had an agreement about what he did when he was on the road. "You don't ask me what I did while you were gone, and if you're stupid enough to get caught, you're in trouble." With men, it's usually a one-night stand with a stranger. When women at home stray, they tend to turn to a friend.

But we're still together today, more vital than ever, more than 45 years later.

16

A Clash of Raptors

Raptor:
 A carnivorous predatory bird, an eagle, or a hawk at the top of the food chain.

It happened suddenly in July of 1980. I couldn't tell you the exact date. But it was the last show the Eagles, the band as I knew them, would ever do. Though none of us behind the amp line knew it at the time.

We sensed a storm was brewing. Everything was still in a holding pattern two hours after the show was scheduled to begin. The band had not come out of their dressing-room. Even the great Irving Azoff could not get them to budge.

There were muffled shouts, threats, and epithets, coming from the dressing room. A war was raging, and the rest of us wanted no part of it for fear of being collateral damage. Raptors were on the attack, beaks sharpened, talons extended for the kill. They were eating their young.

Rumor backstage was Henley and Frey were arguing with Felder about leaving the band over the fifty dollars more than Felder that Joe Vitale had asked for to do a second show, though Felder had actually been with the band longer. This didn't make sense to us. In our minds, Vitale had to be making enough that fighting over fifty dollars wasn't worth the battle it would take to get it. The rumor proved not to be true. When the delay crept past the two-hour mark, we all looked at each other, wondering if we'd still have jobs in the morning.

It was common knowledge that the band occasionally squabbled amongst themselves. Mostly when there was white powder present. There had always been tension between Frey and Henley and Felder. Frey and Henley were the Eagles. Cut and dry, simple as that.

Joe Walsh had marquee value and credibility as a musical entity and a star in his own right. He was also a complete team player on the Eagles roster. By all accounts, the others were a supporting cast, excellent players in an ensemble cast, very accomplished in their own right, but not the founding fathers and majority "shareholders" of the group.

One point of contention between Frey and Felder was that Glenn occasionally came up with parts that his fingers just couldn't play. While Glenn was the consummate creator, Felder was the consummate player. Everyone on the stage conceded that technically "Fingers" Felder was the best musician on the stage. But Glenn could come up with great guitar parts his fingers couldn't deliver.

Instead of taking Glenn's suggestions in stride, Felder's ego was easily bruised. In his book, *"Heaven and Hell..."* he hinted that he was always hesitant to present songs to Frey and Henley, the principal writers of the band, for fear of being shot down. In their defense, they *had* come up with many classic hits, and Henley was known to be a detail monster that could go through a new song, pick it apart over and over, and rework it in minute detail until it was right for the band. That might intimidate an insecure person.

The band finally found their way to the stage two hours late. Glenn came over to me to get his guitar for the first song.

"I'm gonna kill him."

"Kill who…" I said. "I didn't know what he was talking about. We didn't know. We didn't know they were breaking up."

"Who're you killing?"

"If Felder comes near me, I'm killing Him."

I tried to signal Felder's guy, Jimmy Collins, to let him know, "these two are feuding." It never reached Collins. Later in the show, it got to the point where Felder was starting to wander over into Glenn's turf. I didn't actually hear it from where I was standing behind the amp line, but in Felder's biography, he says that Glenn taunted him during the entire performance by leaning into him and saying, "When this show is over, I'm gonna kick your ass." According to Felder's account, Frey gave him periodic updates during the show, letting him know how many songs were left like, "That's three more, get ready" and "one more song motherfucker, and I'm kicking your ass."

When the show ended, band members made their way to their limo's. Felder asked Jimmy Collins to get him his inexpensive Takamine acoustic guitar. He began waving it around like a Ninja. Then he started banging it against a concrete wall over and over again until it lay broken in pieces on the floor. With unfortunate timing, Alan Cranston, the politician whose rally they were playing, and his wife, rounded the corner. They both stood frozen with looks of abject horror on their faces.

The crew hadn't known it then, but it would be our last show with the Eagles.

I woke up the next morning, unemployed, after years of steady touring.

But the end hadn't begun there. As with all band breakups in that era, the end developed over time as most conflicts do. Egos collide, and borders are violated. Rivalries fester, white powder is consumed. Warning shots are fired that lead to all-out battle. When that happens, few ever leave a rock n roll battlefield whole. Later after the war, the dust settles, and PTSD sets in. Some move on and others retire, many proclaim their independence. Some succeed, others don't and are never heard from again.

I was just proud to have played a small part in the Eagle's most significant era of hit records and sold-out touring shows.

17

Out Of The Ashes: The Glenn Frey Tours

When the Eagles tour ended for good, I was back on the payroll for a short time to sort out all the equipment. Much of it was owned by the group.

I went down to their locker, took it all out, sorted it into piles according to what belonged to each player and what belonged to the group. That was officially the end of my time with the band. They had ceased to exist, but I was still proud of my time with the band.

Glenn Frey had never been one to let moss grow beneath his feet. After all, his drive had been the primary force behind the formation and success of the Eagles. After the Eagles, he continued being productive as a musician and a creator. He had the track record that would allow him to do it at the level he was accustomed to.

Glenn once again came to my rescue. He took me on as a sort of man Friday. I did anything and everything he might need to be done. You might say I was his gofer. But I like to think I was a bit more than that. After all, I was a veteran of the Eagles road tours. I had lived the life and survived the legendary golden era of Eagles touring. At times I was Glenn's friend and confidant, his co-conspirator, trusted employee, and his sounding board as he moved into a new phase in his life, a new phase in both our lives. But this time, I was strictly on Glenn's payroll, and I answered only to him.

It had been a long road For Glenn from his early days in Detroit where he gained his first real rock n roll experiences singing on fellow Detroiter Bob Seger's hit, *Ramblin' Gamblin' Man*. Later, as a member of Linda Ronstadt's band, he worked with future Eagles partner Don Henley and met original Eagles Randy Meisner and Bernie Leadon.

In the new phase of Glenn's career, he produced a girl singer named Lu Ann Barton with the legendary Jerry Wexler. He was also the producer of other acts like LA's *Jack Mack And The Heart Attack*, a kick-ass horn band with a funky sound, and a great drummer, Claude Pepper. He also produced Karla Bonoff and even found time to launch a solo career that had brought forth the hits, *You Belong To The City*, *Smugglers Blues*, and *True Love*, as well as five solo albums including *No Fun Aloud* and *The All-nighters*.

In addition to his music, Glenn also launched a career as an actor on TV shows like *Miami Vice*, *Wiseguy*, *South Of Sunset*, and *Nash Bridges*. He also had parts in the films *Let's Get Harry* and *Jerry Maguire*.

In June of 1982, Glenn's first solo album, No Fun Aloud, was released. The album was very well received, and reviewers around the country praised it. One reviewer in Delaware called it a "low key affair that radiates the enjoyment of someone who has rediscovered his enthusiasm for Music." Glenn was quoted as responding with, "I told myself I'd work on it only when I felt good. With the Eagles, we'd end up booking the studio for four weeks and just stick it out no matter how we felt..."

Though none of his five solo albums would ever make it to the national top 10, things were happening for Glenn on his own, and reviews of his work were excellent. For the next few years, I had steady employment with him on all his projects.

In 1982 we were back on the road again for Glenn's solo tour, opening for Fleetwood Mac in the US and Japan. We did several dates in the US apart from the *Glenn Frey No Fun Aloud Tour tour*. Glenn called the band *The Heaters*.

We did a one-off show in Dublin at The National Stadium, a small arena. Glenn decided that he wanted to record and videotape the performance. That videotaped stand-alone concert came to be known as the Strange Weather Tour. It would also become his best Solo Album of the same name and a tremendous well-produced video of the concert.

Glenn's band on that project included Marty Fera on Drums, Bryan Garofalo on bass, Al Garth on violin and Saxophone, Danny Grenier and Duane Sciacqua on Guitars, Darryl Leonard on trumpet, Chris Mostert on Tenor Sax and Shaker, Barry Sarna and Jay Oliver on Keyboards, Greg "Frosty" Smith on Baritone Sax, and Michito Sanchez on Percussion.

The camera crew had set up a dolly track in front of the stage, and a cameraman rolled back and forth on the dolly the entire width of the stage. For some reason, the cameraman was getting on Glenn's nerves. During the show, Glenn roamed back and forth across the stage. He became more and more irritated with the camera guy. A couple of times, Glenn looked right at him and said, "Stay there, don't follow me. Shoot from the other side."

When I saw what was happening, I ran out from backstage and tapped the cameraman on the shoulder and said, "Hey, calm down, don't follow him, he wants you to shoot from that side. You're pissing him off."

That should actually have been his manager, Peter Lopez's job. Peter, a nice guy, was new to artist management. He might have been a capable attorney and a good deal maker, but he was no Irving Azoff. Peter was a deal maker, not a head breaker. He should have been protecting his client Glenn, in all aspects of his career. Mostly if the client wasn't happy with the way things were going. Glenn was a loyal guy to the people and the things he believed in, and he expected those around him to look out for him as well, and rightfully so.

When Glenn came off the stage at the end of the show, he was still angry. He went right for Peter and began tearing into him. He was screaming at the top of his lungs.

The crowd in the arena was still applauding, but Glenn just kept getting hotter and hotter. Frankly, he was making an ass out of himself, and I knew something had to be done to calm him down. Initially, I had faded into the background, but when I realized this was a bad situation getting worse by the second, I stepped up. Taking my own life in my hands, I interrupted and stepped into the fray.

"So, uh, boss, are we doing an encore?"

I told him we had a job to do in so many words, and it wasn't over yet.

That sort of snapped him back to reality and the business at hand. He looked over at me and said, "Yeah, we'll do an encore." I turned away and yelled out, "Band, places, Glenn, stage, Everyone, encore," and that was the end of that episode.

By interrupting as I did, I probably saved Peter from any further abuse that night, and Glenn didn't fire him. Sadly, not long afterward, Peter committed suicide. His death was not related to Glenn at all. The man was a successful Hollywood attorney. He was most likely under a lot of pressure from all sides.

That was not the first time Glenn acted out. I'd seen it happen before. One night he was unhappy with his Tour manager

Tommy Nixon and threw a full bottle of beer. Granted, it was thrown to miss him, but what if it wouldn't have missed?

Another night when Glenn was on a tear, he proceeded to berate everyone in his sight. I was standing there with a bass guitar in my hand. I'm not a bass player by any means, but I was noodling away on the instrument when Glenn stormed out of the room. I was the only one he hadn't come after. He was halfway out the door, and I thought I was home free. Suddenly he stopped, turned around, and yelled at me, "And you, you can't play bass!" It was almost as if it dawned on him that he had forgotten one person in his tirade, me, and stopped to correct his mistake. But he was right, I couldn't play bass, I could tune one, but I couldn't play it. To me, it had been a convenient prop to vent my nervous energy.

Glenn took everything very seriously, sometimes way too seriously. But I knew him well in the many years I worked for him. Glenn's good side far outweighed the bad, and sometimes with family, you just have to take your lumps in stride and move on.

"On one tour overseas, we found all these little after-hours joints." There was a club we began to frequent where we got to know the bartender pretty well. "We even got him tickets to one of our sold-out shows, and he took good care of us."

We were hanging out there late one night when the bartender sent someone over to us to say, "You better get over here right away, your boy is in trouble." I gathered all our guys together, and we went over to the bar to see what the trouble was. There were three girls at the bar with their boyfriends. Apparently, Duane, one of the band's guitar players, had been hitting on one or all of them. He was really drunk and bragging that he was with "the band." By the time we got there, the girl's dates had started to get a bit riled up over his rude behavior towards their women.

We grabbed Duane and literally pulled him out of the place. We dragged him about five blocks back to the hotel with his feet turned under, the tips of his toes dragging on the ground.

The next day after he'd sobered up, he confronted us and wanted to know what had happened to him the night before. He was really pissed off and said we ruined his shoes. In dragging him back to the hotel, the tips of his shoes had gotten scuffed up and worn down.

On the bus waiting for Glenn to come down, everyone got on him, "How you gonna explain that," we said.

Then Glenn showed up and hid his shoes. The prankster strikes!

After Glenn got off the bus at the next hotel, we explained to him, "We had to drag your sorry ass back to the hotel because you couldn't even walk. We dragged you five blocks, that's why you don't have tips on your shoes. You wanted to fight three guys for their girlfriends. For all you know, they could have been expert Karate guys. We saved your ass."

When we played Madison Square Garden in New York, I had terrible back pains. I was walking bent over with my hands on my knees. The show promoter said bluntly, "What's wrong with you."

I was so bent over I could barely walk. "I need someone that can get me out of this pain," I said, "an acupuncturist, a chiropractor, I don't care, just get me out of this pain. I have a show to do."

He said, "No problem, I've got a guy." When "the guy" showed up, I could barely get on the table. He took a needle and stuck it in my back. Then he moved it around. He put it in several different places. I got some relief, but not much. The next day I woke up, and I was still in pain. So, I went to the promoter again. This time he said, "What's wrong with you, Bob?" I said, "I don't know! If I knew, I wouldn't be in pain."

Then the promoter got me another doctor. The new guy did almost the same treatment as the last one. But he stuck a needle in me, slapped me on my rear, and said, "Did you feel that?" "No," I said. He moved the needle and hit me again, "Feel that?" "Yeah, I felt that," I moaned.

When Glenn came in, I was standing halfway straight again, and he remarked, "You look better." "I know I look a little better," I said, "but I don't feel better." "Let's just do this show," he replied. "We'll get out of here, and you'll get better."

Tony, one of the techs with the show, offered," I'll help out with guitars. I'll just move that one over there and that one over there." I stopped him in mid-sentence. "You can't do that. You can't touch anything here. This is a union house. It's local 1, the strictest union in the country. If you touch something, the stagehands will break us in half. We would never see the equipment again. You and I and the equipment would be floating face down in the Hudson. "They've been known to break out the bats too. We don't need blood on the bats. The blood would be our blood, yours and mine.

The doctor worked on me again and got me standing upright. I still couldn't lift or move anything, but I was feeling better. I found the union steward, pulled him aside, and gave him a thousand dollars of expense money and said, "Spread this around amongst your crew. I want to be out of here two hours after the show ends." He didn't complain. But our crew did. The union crew got bonused, and they didn't. But we kept the peace, and no one ended up in the Hudson.

Glenn enlisted Joe Walsh for an around the world tour. With the names Joe Walsh and Glenn Frey on the marquee, they quickly filled arena's and had some fun playing music again without all the drama that had become the latter days of the Eagles.

No chain saws at 3am, and no individual mattresses carted into hotels for the band members. It was just Joe and Glenn and the band playing music. We were lean and mean, sort of.

Before the tour, Glenn called a production meeting with the staff and the two tour managers. He laid out the ground rules, "No Drinking, no blow, no pot...no nothing on the road. If anyone does anything, I'll cancel the tour." We all nodded our agreement, just happy to be working again.

At one of our first shows, Glenn was onstage opening the show. Joe was about to make his entrance. When he walked by me, I noticed he had a big white powder spot under his nose. I thought, "Oh shit!

I began motioning towards my nose and my upper lip at Joe. He ignored me. I turned to Smokey, his road manager, with a sense of urgency and said, "Smokey, he's got blow under his nose. Smokey answered sternly, "No, he doesn't."

At that point in the show, Glenn introduced Joe, and they'd sit down to play a duet together. Joe walked out with a guitar, as usual, sat down and looked directly at Glenn with the big white spot under his nose. It was practically glowing and blinking like a big neon sign saying, blow, blow, blow.

Glenn looked directly at Joe, then called me out on stage. I could tell he was on the verge of freaking out about it when he said, "After this song, I want everybody in my dressing room immediately."

I got on the walkie talkie and announced, "After the next song, dressing room, all hands needed in the dressing room, after the next song."

Backstage in the dressing room, Glenn launched into all of us. "I told you all no Drinking, no pot, no blow on the tour." Joe, chuckling to himself, answered, "That wasn't blow, that was baby powder... can't take a joke?" The whole room started giggling to themselves then burst out in a fit of laughter, calling out, "You got punked, you got punked." Glenn had always been known as a big prankster. Joe, the Clown Prince Of Rock n Roll, had beat him at his own game.

One New Year's Eve, Glenn wanted to play a small club in Aspen with The Heaters. There was a place he liked in Aspen that he thought would be perfect. It was small and intimate and convenient to his Aspen house where he was staying. (He owned 3 homes in Aspen)

We were at the club as the patrons arrived, sitting at the bar and drinking with Glenn. He was buying, so I was drinking, and we were all pretty much hammered on Peppermint Schnapps. There was a limit on the capacity in the club. We had promised the local fire marshal that we would not go over 300 people. I looked around and noticed that the place was jammed to the rafters. I went to the guy at the door and reminded him that we couldn't go over 300 people. "You have to let me know when we get to that number," I said. He looked right at me and said, "OK, we have 330 people, pick 30 people, and I'll throw them out." "You can't do that…" I said, "just don't let anyone else in. Glenn watched me do my little pony show with the doorman, thinking I'm sure that it would ultimately reflect on him if it got out of hand.

Back at the bar, I resumed hammering down shots of schnapps with Glenn when a man approached us. "Hey Glenn, it's your caretaker, he's in Jail." Glenn looked at me, "How did he end up in Jail." I'm thinking, "Jeesh! World War II was my fault…I wasn't there to stop it." Instead, I said, "I don't know, I didn't lock him up. How do I know how he got there? I'm here with you."

"Well we gotta go get him," Glenn said,

We'd been drinking schnapps and Heineken all night. We were still really hammered. Glenn had been buying, so I'd been drinking. Regardless, with no attempt to sober up, we managed to get out of the club and into a cab and make our way to the police station. Glenn showed his face, laid down the cash, and we got the caretaker out in short order. Not long after that, Glenn fired the caretaker. I didn't ask why.

Glenn Frey Tours

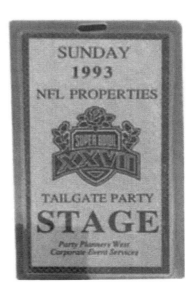

Glenn and Cindy's Wedding in Aspen, Colorado

The Monstertones

More Crew Fun on The Long Run Tour - New opening act

18

Doug's Place

If someday a monument to roadies, the unsung heroes of rock n roll, should ever be built, I'd nominate one person whose name should be inscribed in stone at its base. He didn't tour with the bands, he wasn't a tour manager or a production manager, sound engineer, or lighting tech, and he didn't drive the truck or the bus. In fact, he wasn't even a "roadie" in the strictest definition of the term. But he was known and loved by roadies one and all that ever knew him, and most of us knew him or knew of him, and he helped every last one of us. He was far from a perfect human being. But he was a one of a kind character with a great heart and the rock n roll spirit and work ethic that was woven in the fabric of the music scene in LA in the 1970s and early '80s. Sadly, in his final years, he was chased by demons. Yet Doug Smalley was legendary and loved by all who made his acquaintance.

There have been rehearsal facilities in Hollywood for as long as there has been an entertainment business. In the early days, none were large enterprises, and many were located in television and movie studios across town. Fox studios had a few, and at NBC TV studios in Burbank, there were several. One of the first in Hollywood was used by musical artists to rehearse for their tours in the 1960s. It was located on the second floor of a building next to the Capitol Records tower on Vine Street. Before that, most musical artists rehearsed at the musician's union farther south on Vine Street. The union had several rehearsal rooms used by everyone from big bands, session players, crooners, and early rock n rollers.

In the late nineteen sixties, the Beatles revolutionized the industry, and the number of successful rock bands grew. Rock n roll touring became an industry unto its own. Bands have always had someone, a guy that set up the stage. Big bands called them "band boys." They came into a venue and set up the music stands and set out the sheet music books. In the early days of rock n roll, the bands didn't call us "roadies," we were called "equipment managers." A good guess is that the term "roadie" may have come over with the British Invasion groups of the early 1960s.

With the expansion of the rock n roll industry, rental equipment and rehearsal space became a need. Studio Instrument Rentals in Hollywood was the first to do it on a grand scale. They did cartage of instruments around town and rented gear to musicians, record producers, film and recording studios, and countless others, anyone who needed to rent or move musical instruments. A natural result of their success was their expansion into the rehearsal studio business. Rock n roll touring had become huge, and there was a need for dedicated space where amplifiers and other electric instruments could have access to AC power and a small PA system to rehearse a tour and polish the act, so to speak. A place where no neighbors would complain of the "noise" and musicians coming and going at all hours. Eventually, by the early 1970s, SIR had established themselves as the leaders in that niche market of the entertainment business. Soon others followed suit. Rock n roll was here to stay and had become a significant money maker. Soon other rental and cartage companies came along. Many had at least one studio for rent on their premises.

By the mid-1970s, rock tours went big into production, and more space was needed for rehearsals. SIR expanded into several larger areas that included at least one defunct film studio. A band or artists crew could put up their entire arena touring rig, sound, lights, staging equipment, and rehearse with it as it would be set up on tour. At that time, at that level, they were the only game in rock n roll tour rehearsals.

I met Doug in the early 1970s. He was a nice young man of the post counterculture generation, hip, and clean-cut, with a job. He lived in the nearby Hollywood Hills with his sweet young bride in a quaint little house, more of a cabin, with a view. They were a cute little post-hippie generation couple, farm fresh from Nebraska. In their own organic world, they had a loving relationship in the Hollywood hills amid the leafy trees and lush plant life on the hillsides. They lived far above the concrete and asphalt and the dark corners of Hollywood of the 1970s. They hadn't been in LA long. Not long enough to be lured into the dark side of Hollywood.

Doug worked for SIR at their main rehearsal and rental complex on Sunset Boulevard. I'd worked the streets doing studio cartages in Hollywood and around town and occasionally crossed paths with their cartage guys at various studios. But I never saw Doug on the trucks. As far as I knew, he worked strictly in the rehearsal halls dispatching rentals and doing setups and teardowns.

At some point, SIR expanded again to a new facility. It was off the beaten path in a seedy part of Hollywood across from the Hollywood Forever Cemetery, one of the oldest cemeteries in Los Angeles known for the celebrities of Hollywood's Golden age like Douglas Fairbanks and Rudolph Valentino that are buried there.

The facility was a repurposed beverage distributors warehouse on Santa Monica Blvd. in Hollywood, not far from SIR's main facilities. In size, it was somewhere between their medium-sized rooms and the high square footage of the old movie studio. It was the perfect place to rehearse. It was just far enough away from the main drags of Hollywood. Officially it was called Studio Six, but we referred to it as Doug's Place after Doug Smalley, the manager, facilitator, and at times a full-time resident of the premises. Every roadie in the business had loaded their artists show into Doug's place at one time or another. We loved it for

159

its privacy, its huge loading dock, and because Doug, though he'd never been on the road, was one of us.

Not long after I met Doug, he and his wife split up, and it nearly killed him. Gone was the clean-cut, nice guy I had become acquainted with. He was sullener and moodier. Somehow, he got SIR owners to allow him to create living quarters for himself on the premises. He began living his work 24/7.

In his heart, Doug was still a good guy, but he had gone Hollywood. Not the glitz and glamor Hollywood of fame, but the Hollywood of the streets south of Sunset Blvd. He was a quick study, and though he had many friends amongst us, Doug watched his back and took no crap. Doug's closest and best friend and constant companion was his dog, Haywire.

Doug assimilated into the noir side of Hollywood, the mean streets of Sam Spade, Mike Hammer, and Phillip Marlowe, where sleazy characters roamed after dark, lurking in dim-lit doorways and roosting in tacky low rent fast food joints and Taco stands. Three large city blocks north, Hollywood Blvd. had a sleazy but legendary charm of former opulence. But the environs around Doug's place were of pure urban decay.

After studio hours, Doug's place was a party, and everyone that hung out there brought something to the mix. It was central casting for roadies, working, and not. A place where the camaraderie of the road carried over into real life. It was a rock n roll version of a VFW hall for veterans of the road. It was a place where veterans gathered, got high, and told war stories with other kindred spirits.

Everyone that ever rehearsed at studio six adored Doug, and everyone came back sooner or later, even as he slipped farther and farther into the abyss of whatever stormy seas he was drowning in in his head.

We all had Doug stories, and each of us had pounded on his door on a given morning for what seemed like an eternity until he dragged himself, literally screaming and moaning to the door, often half-clothed and hungover, and once or twice wholly naked. Sometimes we had well-known artists in tow. I've banged on his door until my fist hurt. One of my colleagues, tired of banging with his fist, kicked the aluminum bottom of the plate glass door, slipped, and put his foot through the glass. Somehow that got Doug's attention and woke him. On numerous occasions, I made excuses to my rock star bosses as to why we couldn't get into a rehearsal hall we were paying for by the hour.

But as roadies, we were professionals, touring veterans. We got that the days were long, and the sleep was short, and the mornings could be grubby when we were hungover. But it wasn't supposed to be like that at home. When it came time to do the work, we showed up on time, ready to rock, with enthusiasm, regardless of the condition of our minds or the environment around us. Doug's behavior would not have been tolerated on tour. But we loved Doug, and we made excuses for him, and we often had to call the main building to get someone with a key to open up for us and drag his ass out of bed.

Doug had become the Charles Bukowski of studio managers. Bukowski was a talented LA poet and a short story writer, a drunk, and a novelist. He wrote about the underbelly of Los Angeles and lived the life of a low-life bar fly and cheap womanizer. He is known for works like "Bar Fly" and "*Love Is A Dog From Hell.*"

Doug's life took another turn for the worse after the suicide of his friend. Doug found the remains. His friend's body was severely damaged after shooting himself in the head with a shotgun. It has been described by others as a "bloody mess" with "splatter all over the walls and floor." Doug's life went further downhill after that.

But Doug continued to run the studio and party there after hours. I can still see him running out of a half set up studio with his hair on fire after answering an urgent call from a rock idol that kept his gear in a locker at the facility.

"Where you goin' Dougie, we're not done yet!"

"I gotta get a fed ex off to an artist at his farm, I can't talk now," he'd say, his voice trailing off as he ran to the musician's locker to get some mysterious item rock stars can't live without.

Doug was known to barge in on an artist's session and announce, "Rehearsals over, I have another group coming in, in one hour, everyone out!"

Doug's dog "Haywire" had been his loyal companion for years. Toward the end of his life, Haywire could barely walk. Doug would back his car into the loading bay and open the hatchback where Haywire lay on a doggie mattress scarcely alive. He carried him in and set him behind the counter of the little office he had outside the studios. After Haywire died, Dougie soon followed.

On the day it happened, Doug followed his former roommate's last footsteps into the afterlife, wherever that is, by killing himself with a shotgun. Word spread like wildfire by word of mouth, no social media, no texts, no tweets. But we all found out quickly, and we all silently wept and thought, "Why, Dougie...why?" Can anyone's life be that bad that it has to end like that? I reckoned that Doug never knew how much his friends thought of him and how much he was really loved and appreciated.

In the way of men, we had always shown our love for Doug. We tolerated his inadequacies and foul-ups, we covered for him and had his back, and we accepted him as our own. Not many people that never rode the bus or toured with the big show or saw the world touring in rock n roll have ever been accepted by "us." We are the fraternity of road dogs that have been there and done that. We proudly collect our all-access laminates from the tours we've worked, and we wear the band swag, and we rarely let outsiders in. But we let Dougie in. I don't know how many of us of that era are still alive. But of those I know of, we'll all remember Doug, and we'll all tell our Doug stories until there are none of us left who remember.

If you would have told me then that I would someday be in Doug's shoes and that I could make a go of it with a rehearsal studio of my own. I would have called you crazy. "What, and give up touring?"

But things change, and life goes on, and we learn from the mistakes and the shortcomings of others. And my time would come.

19

Third Encore (3E)

By the time The Eagles ended, I'd worked with many bands and toured overseas with some of them. But I covered most of the globe with the Eagles, the band that sold more records than any other rock n roll band in history. In my time with The Eagles, they were at the peak of their creativity, virtuosity, and popularity.

I was a small part of their most successful live touring shows, and I witnessed the last encore of their Greatest era, and I had capitalized on the experience I got with them. But by the time I began touring and working with Glenn full time, I had grown weary of it and thought it was time to move on.

One day I came home and announced to Toni that Teddy, another roadie friend, and I had been talking. "We want to open up a rehearsal facility in LA" I didn't expect Toni to balk at the idea. I had been involved in other ventures before. I'd built them up, sold them off, then moved-on after I realized that I didn't really care about the business. But I had found my calling in rock n roll, and I loved it. By that time, I had excellent credentials and didn't want to leave touring behind entirely. But I was looking for a way to get off the road. I was beginning to burn out.

Toni sort of took it all in stride. She had concerns about us finding the money. She didn't have a clear picture of how we could do it. But I was jazzed. I said, "Toni, I've been in every shit hole venue and rehearsal hall in the world, and I know how to do it and make it work. I want to build it, and I want to do it right."

I had trust in my abilities, and I knew I could do it better than it had ever been done before. I found a realtor and began looking at properties. There wasn't a lot of money, only about thirty-four thousand dollars. Teddy said he could match it, and we would have equal shares.

An empty building on Vanowen Street not far from Burbank airport was ideal. The Realtor was eager to move it and made me a slam dunk deal. He even threw in the first three months' rent-free. Teddy and I were determined to make it work.

Luckily for us, Teddy's brother-in-law was in construction. He was a framer, just the guy we needed most at that time. The office was already intact, so we began construction on three rooms, studio's A, B, and C.

As fate would have it, a client materialized out of the blue while we put the finishing touches on our first room. An artist's tour manager showed up on our doorstep, looking for rehearsal space for his artist and band. He said they were tentatively booked at another facility across town and had lost their booking. They were in a bind.

"When do you need it," I asked.

"In a few weeks," he said.

"Give me a solid date,"

He shot me a date and said, "Will you be ready by then?"

"I'll tell you what," I said. "If we aren't ready by then, I'll find a place for you, and I'll pay for it."

The artist was Tina Turner.

Later Teddy came to me privately and said, "Do you know what you just did?" I said, "Yeah, I know what I just did, but can we do it?"

Then we actually did it. We had no doors on the women's restrooms, but we did it. We hung shower curtains in the doorways until the doors could be installed.

At nine o'clock on the first day of the Tina Turner rehearsal, Teddy and I were standing at the load-in door. Twenty minutes later, there was still no truck, and we looked at each other, wondering if we'd been had. Then a truck showed up, followed by the tour manager. He explained the truck had been lost with apologies. He had to lead them to the facility.

That first room was one hundred percent complete, but the others were still under construction. Luckily the completed room had access from the outside. To get to it, you didn't have to go through the rest of the building at all. Tina Turner and company never had to be anywhere near the construction and drywall dust. Apparently, the rehearsals went well because Tina Turner became our first- and long-time client.

Once the other two rooms were completed, we decided to host a grand opening. Harry McCarthy, the owner of Drum Paradise, now a successful business in Nashville, brought in his band. With the addition of two other local bands, we had one in each studio. We brought in beer and sodas and deli-trays, standard open house fare in rock n roll. We didn't think anyone would come, but we were gonna go for it anyway.

Toni and I lived a few minutes away in North Hollywood. We left the house early to get to the open house and couldn't figure out why there was so much traffic at that time in North Hollywood. As it turned out, all that traffic was going to Third Encore.

Tina Turner and her group, our first clients, came in and professionally went about their business. Our policy was to not interfere or get personally involved with the clients. "We never crashed anyone's party." They rented the studio, and as far as we were concerned, it was sovereign territory, as an embassy in a foreign country. It was their turf for as long as they rented it.

One morning, I was sitting in the office when I heard Rickie Lee Jones in the hall outside her studio yelling for me, "Norton, Norton." I ran out of the office and found her in the hallway. She was screaming my name. I could hear the band in the next room, cranking at volume level "eleven." She immediately tore into me, screaming, "I can't rehearse here, listen to that music." Truth told, they were louder than she could ever play over, and why would she ever want to.

Rickie Lee was really freaking out. She was so mad she scared me, and I don't scare easy. When your client freaks out, that's when you just have to calm yourself, take your lumps and keep your wheels turning toward finding a solution, which I soon came up with. Once she was settled down, I went into the other studio and approached the band with a proposition. I said, "Look, it's a bit loud for the artist next door, but I'll do you a favor. You knock off for a while and come back at six this afternoon, and I'll give you the room for free. The room next door will be empty, and all in all, you will have gotten about ten hours for the cost of four." Without hesitation, they accepted. And they say metal-heads are burnouts!

I went back to Rickie, and she was happy again. Then she fired her percussion player, who just happened to be her husband. All problems solved.

The incident with Rickie Lee raised another issue. When Teddy and I built 3E, we made the studios back to back with no insulated air gap between them. From the Rickie Lee incident, we learned the problems that could cause. After that, we built an insulated gap between all the studios. We ended up losing about a foot and a half in each room, but it really didn't matter.

Paula Abdul rented a room for three months. She bought everyone beautiful black leather backpacks as a thank-you. Her management paid the bill on time every time, and I have to say that it was pretty standard for our clients, with a few exceptions.

Milli Vanilli, a German group, came in to rehearse one year around Christmas. They were a duo, two lead singers, and a backup band, and they were successful at the time. Their careers were peaking, and they had sold millions of records. During rehearsals, they gave their band off for Christmas, and we shut down 3E for that holiday as well.

I got a call at home from them on Christmas Day. They said they had to rehearse. I was home with my family, my relatives were over, and we were enjoying the holiday. I said, "It's going to be expensive; I have to call in a guy to open up and be there for you. I ended up being that guy. I charged them a ridicules hourly amount for the inconvenience."

When I opened up for them, there were just the two principals of the group and someone that looked more like a businessman or a manager. They stayed for two hours. When they were leaving, I asked, "Have you finished already." The answer was, "Yes, we just needed a place to meet."

Shortly after that meeting, their agent confessed publicly that the two principals did not sing any of the vocals heard on their music releases. The duo ended up giving back their Grammy award for Best New Artist. They recorded another album that tanked, then one of the duo passed away, and that was the end of Milli Vanilli.

Later we had the artist Yanni in one of the studios. He had a large band with three keyboard players. He was a decent guy.

When he came in, he always made a point of saying hello to myself and Toni and the staff. We appreciated that.

Another keyboard player, Hollywood based, originally from Iowa, was the son of a music store owner. He had a locker at 3E. He had gotten into synthesizers early-on when they were still new and had a huge ego about it. He was among the few synth specialists that did big recording sessions around town, and he was a real pain.

We offered him the locker he wanted for the standard price that everyone, rich or poor, famous or unknown, paid for theirs. We had a set price on all the lockers, but he came back at us with half that price and insisted that we give him the space for his price. After pushing and pestering us, I had to tell him in no uncertain terms that if he didn't like the price, he was free to go somewhere else, no harm, no foul. But he wouldn't give up. He kept pestering us like a two-year-old at a supermarket check-out counter.

Lockers were the same price for everyone, and I held the line. He drove me so nuts I bluntly explained it to him again and showed him the door. A band he toured with briefly had an affectionate nickname for him having to do with a male anatomy appendage. Apparently, he was in demand in the studio but had failed to make any friends among his fellow musicians. Eventually, he caved-in and reluctantly rented the locker. He ended up running a keyboard-related business from that locker as well.

Then there was Ozzy.

Ozzy Osborn was a truly unique and strange individual.
Toni Said about Ozzy:

"At first, when I was in the front office, Ozzy sometimes came in and talked to me. I have never looked into a person's eyes and not seen anything. He scared me... I couldn't even talk to him. Ozzy's eyes were completely dead. He'd come in to rehearse in a robe and slippers and pajama bottoms. He shuffled through the halls like an old man in a nursing home."

"That's where I got my pajama thing on tour from.

He'd come in my office and say, 'Norton, let's go have a cigarette.' I'd say, 'Ozzy, I don't smoke,' and he'd always reply with,' well, come watch me smoke.' This went on all day long. He wouldn't talk to me; he wouldn't say anything. I don't know... in his mind, maybe I was like his personal roadie or something. It was wild. Otherwise, he was a nice guy, personable. He signed a poster about four feet by two feet, To Norton, thanks for everything, Ozzy."

Ozzy's guitar player collected little characters of wrestlers. He had them all over his amp. "Every day, I brought in a new wrestling character and placed it on his amp. When he came in, he'd stare at the amp and study it, trying to figure out what was different. Then he'd see that he had one extra wrestler. It was a game we both enjoyed."

When Ozzie came in, I'd have to take him outside for his smoke break around the corner where no one could see him. Ozzie was really crazy. He was even crazier than Joe Walsh and made Brian Wilson look downright sane.

Ozzy pulled no punches. For example, if someone of status like a Tina Turner came in, Ozzy would walk up to them, no matter who they were, and say, "Oy, how the fuck are you." He spared no expletives.

Guns and Roses rented a studio for twenty-four-hours a day for three months. Individual band members would show up and stay for a while, and then leave. Slash showed up once. "I saw him there once."

They brought in tapestries and couches and carpets and really decked out the studio. They made it a really cool Guns n Roses environment. It was their own unique space, but they never rehearsed.

Toni:

"Rock n Roll had a lot of money back then. Poison, Brett Michaels, came in for about two or three weeks. No one came in to rehearse for a day or two. Our daily fee didn't hurt their pockets one bit. Poison decided to shoot part of their video at 3E on the handicap ramp we had to put in later after the fact, to comply with the Americans with disabilities act.

Brett Michaels had on a really lovely Poison Jacket, and I told Bobby how much I liked it. Bobby mentioned it to Brett Michaels, and after the video shoot, he gave it to me. I still have it. It's brand new. Later, he used our studios in Nashville, and I'd remind him, 'I still have that jacket'"

173

Brett was a nice guy. His whole band was very nice. But we took outstanding care of everyone that came in to rehearse. That was our job. Even Don Henley liked it, and Henley could be hard to please at times.

When LL Cool J came in, his dad was the main guy. He was both a manager and road manager. He bought all the equipment for the band, the best of everything. If the guitar player needed a new guitar, he bought it.

At one point, he called the band together in their room. He didn't want to pay them. I was standing out in the hallway where I could hear all this yelling and shouting. I was thinking, "What the heck is going on, what happened?" So, I went to LL's dad, Joe, and I said, "Joe, what's going on, Is everything OK?" He said, "These guys want me to pay them." He was surprised that they wanted to be paid. It wasn't like, "These guys did a lousy job," He just didn't want to pay them.

"Then, Teddy and I tried to collect what he owed us. We couldn't get paid either." Joe said, "Come to the hotel, and I'll pay you." So, I went to the hotel where they were staying. Joe put a gun on the table, but I got paid. Joe was a gangster, not a "gangsta," a GANGSTER.

I don't think Joe ever believed his son could be as successful as he became. But when he opened up, he couldn't do anything wrong. He had a room at 3E for weeks and weeks.

"The Jacksons, the original group with Michael, were a

nightmare. A bloody nightmare! First off, the production manager asked if I would cut a hole in the wall adjacent to the stage and add a door. Michael wanted to be able to have his driver pull right up to that door so that he could step out of the limo and be right on the stage." Michael, they said, would pay the cost of installing the door. So, I had a door installed. Afterward, when Michael came in, he walked right out on to the stage as requested.

The Jacksons were rehearsing for an upcoming tour. "One would go in, then come out, another would go in, then leave. Then another would go in. I couldn't keep up. It seemed like they rehearsed one at a time. It went on like that for the whole time. But they had a good band."

Toni, our bookkeeper then, said:

"I was the bookkeeper, and I was asking for money we were due. But they just blew us off. We were dealing with their management…and they were not paying us anything. They were up to about eleven thousand dollars past due. $11K was a pretty good sum for us back then."

When they finished rehearsing, they headed off on tour, and we still had not been paid. We knew their itinerary and knew what flight they were on, and which airlines. We had their gear, and it was scheduled to be dropped curbside at LAX the next morning by one of our trucks.

I cornered Teddy, "We gotta get our money. They owe us eleven thousand dollars. We've got to get it before they get the gear, or we'll never see it."

I walked into their business management company first thing the next morning and said to the girl in reception, "I need to see the Jacksons manager." I got the standard answer, "Do you have an appointment?" I quickly snapped back, "No, I have their equipment." She answered, "Just a minute, let me see if I can find someone."

A few minutes later, the business manager came out. I said, "I have the Jacksons equipment, they're at the airport waiting for it, and I need the money they owe us before it moves."

"We'll mail you a check," he said.

"You'll give me the money now, or they don't get the equipment," I answered. "And the Jacksons can't play without their equipment. You understand that, right?"

A few minutes later, I had a check in hand. I went down to the lobby and gave the check to Teddy and said, "Go to the bank and cash this check right now."

Teddy confirmed a short time later that the check was good, and he had the cash in hand. Our truck was waiting off-site at the airport, and as soon as we got the word, we notified him that it was OK to drop it. Just to be sure, the driver said, "You sure it's OK to drop the gear at the curb?" "Yes, I said, do it."

I thought Teddy was going to drop a turd. Neither he nor his wife ever imagined seeing eleven thousand dollars in cash in their lives, let alone holding it in their hands. That was a considerable amount of money for them.

It's sad to have to resort to those kinds of tactics to get what is legitimately owed you. But we did what we had to do to keep our business, our employees, our livelihood, and our self-respect alive and afloat.

A band that became very popular for a short time rehearsed in one of our studios for a while. They were the twin sons of the legendary Rick Nelson. They called themselves Nelson. At the same time, an all-girl band called The Vixens rehearsed down the hall. The Vixens had become successful as part of the Los Angeles glam metal scene. Some referred to them as female Bon Jovi's.

The hallway at 3E was a popular gathering place for the artists on their breaks. The two groups met in the hallway outside their respective studios.

Soon after the Nelson brothers met two of the Vixens, both bands called it quits for the day. It was late, and we saw the two bands leaving, so we began to lock up for the day as usual. Unbeknownst to us, the brothers and the two girls from Vixen had crept back into the brother's studio as soon as their band members left.

I stuck my head in the studio and unconsciously reached for the light switch as I did every night at that time. Immediately someone yelled out, "Hey!" I turned toward the sound, and there were the two Nelsons and two of the Vixens deeply involved in the act of copulation.

Embarrassed, I bumbled out something like, "Sorry, Sorry," then went out and stood in the hall. They never missed a beat, so to speak, and kept at it until they were finished. Then they all walked out. They passed me and went out of the door without a glance in my direction or a single word.

The next day when the brothers came in, they said, "You didn't tell anybody what happened, did you?" "No, I haven't said a word," I said, But I figure now, about seventeen years later, the statute of limitations has long since run out.

Occasionally we had young people with degrees from technical schools come in to apply for jobs. One was called Full Sail University. I'm not knocking them; it's a great place to begin to learn the basics.

In my opinion, you can't learn about live sound engineering from a university. Mostly they teach how to identify each component, it's purpose, how to turn the system on and off, and troubleshoot any electronic problems.

No school can teach you how to hear music and the spoken word. Nor can it teach you how to work the frequencies and "mix" them together, so they mesh like two synchronized gear wheels one into the other to eliminate the "grinding and clashing" of sound waves. No school can teach you how to do that, let alone how to do it in the middle of an audience of thousands of screaming fans while your artist is screeching into a mic at high decibel levels. And for sure, no school can prepare you for the grueling ordeal that is touring on the road. Only a handful of people can endure the high energy fast-paced schedule of touring. You work fifteen or sixteen hours a day, sleep in a bunk on a bus and wake up at the loading dock of the next venue, 350 or 500 miles down the road, then do it all over again every night for weeks at a time. And dealing with the eccentricities and demands of an artist, tactfully and positively, is an art form that is an essential part of the job.

If you can do all of that and keep your focus and your cool when all about you are losing theirs, then and only then do you qualify for the job.

20

One Door Closes...

"Get over it... Get over it..."

3E was doing well. So well, in fact, that we wanted to expand into another adjacent building. What we needed was cash, and Teddy and I were tapped out. All of our money was tied up in the business. Enter Hans.

Hans was a soundman that had toured with a few acts. He was then a small-time sound company owner, an offshoot of a business he had initially started with a British friend of ours. Our British friend was a person of high integrity that we all knew and loved. Somehow Hans had squeezed our friend out of the partnership in the business he and Hans had started together. Their parting had been far less than amiable. In fact, it left our friend angry and bitter towards him.

Despite the bad reviews on Hans, we still needed cash, and he was there with an offering, so we took it. Hans was now our partner in 3E for better or for worse. It turned out to be worse than worse for me.

Several months later, we expanded out to an additional two rooms in a building across the parking lot and were booked solid. One evening Hans and Teddy and their wives went out to dinner. Hans was promoting the idea, in so many words, that I was wrong for the partnership. But Most of our business had come through me and my relationships with people all across the entertainment business. I had picked a great staff and brought in many of the friends I made in the industry over the years. Most of it was repeat business. We had become a significant factor in the music and touring industry mostly on my personality. Realistically I was a go-getter, and Teddy was not, and Hans? Hans was a slug that left a slimy trail across every garden path he crossed.

Teddy was mainly motivated by his devotion to a wife that egged him on with a fanatical craving for immediate gratification. With her, it wasn't about the long-term success of the business. It was about the instant gratification of short-term cash in hand to buy pretty shiny things at Walmart, and the feel of greenbacks in her hand. She could never grasp the difference between the money in your pocket and acquired wealth. Both she and Teddy were short-sighted and petty.

I came in on a Monday morning buzzing and eager to take on another week. I was proud to be one of the owners of a flourishing business that had gotten the attention of every successful, established, and up and coming touring organization in LA. The business had grown steadily since we opened the doors, actually, from before the doors were officially open. The sky was the limit. As far as I was concerned, by serving our clients at home as well as we'd did on tour, we could quickly get over, above, and beyond that limit.

Hans and Teddy called a meeting in Hans' office to drop a bomb on me. "I'm thinking, maybe they have some new ideas on how we can add another studio or double the number of lockers. I liked lockers, no overhead, steady money every month, no labor involved, and little or no maintenance. I was ready. I was always ready for something new."

Hans, the spokesman, said, "We want you out of the business." I'd been blindsided. "You want *me* out of the business, *me?*" I said. Then I looked right at Teddy and said, "You going along with this shit? We started this business together."

Teddy's mumbled answer was timid and whiny. "Well, we don't get paid every week, and Hans and I…" I interrupted, "Oh, it's Hans and me now. You mean that piece of shit," I said, pointing at Hans. "If you needed money, you should have spoken up. I would have found the money for you."

Then Hans interjected. "We'll give you $60K and buy you out." I was angry. I stood up and walked out of the room and immediately called my lawyer. My attorney said, "Don't take $60K, tell them you want $80K".

I went back in and spat out "$80K, take it or leave it!" Then it was Hans' turn to whine. He sounded like a fourth grader when he said, "But the number is $60K." He was stupid enough to think that I would bow to his command. He had no clue that I'd come back at him with a higher number. It was suddenly clear to me that I had been dealing with a couple of real rocket scientists all along.

Hans pathetically whined back, "I can't give you $80K."

"Then you can't buy me out, I said. Let me buy you two idiots out. I'll give you each $50K." Hans wriggled in his seat like the worm he is, trying to escape a hot can. He knew he was stuck and couldn't get out of the deal. In the end, I settled for the $80K, went into my office, packed up my things, and never looked back.

On the way to the door, everyone, the entire staff and crew that I hand-picked wanted to know what was going on. I told them, "I was bought out by Hans and Teddy, they don't want me to be part of 3E anymore, so they bought me out."

Then staff and crew members chimed in, "I'm not staying either." Or, "I'm gone too." Most of the staff was following me out the door when Hans stuck his head out and said, "You can't take those people with you!" To which I answered, "I'm not taking anyone 'with me,' they're leaving because they want to leave." One crew member had a change of heart and went back. Last I heard, he was still there after 23 years and two changes of ownership.

Teddy and his wife's main issue was that Teddy had charge of a separate enterprise within the company, the cartage business. What neither he nor his wife could ever grasp was that cartages, as well as studio rentals, are billed by invoice. Invoices are most often paid by big entertainment companies within thirty days of receipt of the invoice. Pretty standard for most businesses.

I think Teddy and his wife had it in their minds that the business end was like the ice cream man driving through the neighborhood ringing his little bell and collecting nickels and dimes and dollar bills from the kids. You know the guy. The one with the little silver change machine on his belt and a cigar box full of currency. I'm convinced they thought *cash* came in immediately, and they could just get a fistful of money when it suited them, shove it in their wallets and spend it like kids on a buying spree at a Seven-Eleven.

Like I said, rocket scientists.

They say, "If you lie down with dogs, you get fleas." Predictably Hans eventually bought out Teddy. I have little doubt that he most likely low-balled Teddy like he tried to low-ball me. Knowing Teddy like I do, it would be a good bet that he caved in immediately for some fast cash. Everyone I knew (our English friend, Teddy, and Me) that ever got involved in business with Hans left with a bad taste in their mouths and a much thinner wallet.

Years later, Teddy showed up in Nashville at the peak of our success and ask to see my new facility that was the talk of the music community. I had no desire to re-live his betrayal, one that history had proven was ill-advised.

Toni wasn't that involved in the day to day at 3E, but she says:

When Bobby and Teddy had 3E, I would go in once or twice a week to do the books. I worked full time for a company called Embassy Auctioneers, on Ventura Blvd at Reseda Blvd. They were owned by an Israeli couple. They had people in New York that shipped them beautiful handmade expensive rugs, cheaper rugs of all kinds, and diamonds of varying qualities from the best to mediocre. They had fifty-seven auctioneers that flew out to different locations to hold auctions. They also owned an apartment building where they housed a Mexican immigrant labor force that worked in the warehouse. The Mexicans were decent and pleasant to work with, but they had to live like cockroaches, six or seven of them in each of those little apartments. He ended up giving them one of his old Mercedes.

Our house in North Hollywood had become party central. Everybody loved Bobby and would show up after baseball games and at all hours to hang out and drink margaritas, get high, and swim in our pool. We were trying to be a family, and it got old, really quick. Not long after 3E opened, we moved out to Palmdale, a far suburb about 45 minutes north of LA. Another reason was that there was a wave of shooters targeting cars on the freeways during that time. It had gotten scary in town.

I continued to work at Embassy. I did all the advertising for them. I typed up all the ads and sent them in to the newspapers. I also did all the out of town hotel bookings for the auctioneers.

When I told the Embassy owners about Bobby's situation with Teddy and Hans, they said, "Why don't we buy it. We'll give

Bobby $150K and a nice salary to run the place, and you'll work for us. We'll keep it in our little family." That gave Bobby a lot of leverage. When he went back to Hans and Teddy, he had a $150K offer to buy them out in his pocket. He said if they didn't come up with the $80K in 30 days, he would buy 3E from *them*. That called their bluff. They came up with it in the stipulated 30 days, and Bobby walked away from everyone, free and clear with $80K and no partners.

Embassy did an auction in Las Vegas, and I went there to help with writing up all the tickets. We had advertised it like crazy.

Bobby was a shill in the audience. We did well there and cleared about $200K.

Glenn was sort of on hiatus, but Bobby was still on retainer for a while. Then Glenn dropped the retainer, and with 3E out of the picture, Bobby had time on his hands, so he became an auctioneer for a time. He'd fly out every weekend and work as an auctioneer. I'd fly out with him and do the books and collect the money. I knew the business, and Bobby had a code for every item that showed what it cost. He just had to make a profit. We did that for about 3 months.

When we lived in North Hollywood, the lady next door absolutely loved our daughter Summer. Summer would stay with her on the weekends. She was a gem. She warmed up Summers bath towels and made her favorite foods, and we really trusted her.

We also sold t-shirts at concerts for a time. We sold at the Forum, Irvine Meadows, Long Beach, and other significant venues, and made ten percent of the table. On one Prince concert, we made about $1000 in one night. We bought our house in Palmdale from that, but it wasn't easy. We were both still working for the auctioneers. We'd sell late at concerts, then get up early to go to our regular jobs. It was a real grind until something better suited to us came along.

21

Nashville Sound Check

Toni and I continued doing auctions and selling t-shirts, burning the candle at both ends, trying to make a buck, and I still worked for Glenn. Then the something better we were looking for actually did come along.

Glenn and I were talking one day, and he asked me what had happened with Third Encore. "They tried to screw me is what happened," I said. "Teddy and Hans tried to buy me out with a lowball offer, and I turned the tables on them. In the end, they gave me my price, and I walked away."

"What are you gonna do?" he answered.

"Unless you're firing me, I'm gonna keep working for you when you work."

"Do you know anything about that business?" Glenn said.

"Yeah, I know everything about that business."

"Where can you build another one?"

"There are only a few places on earth where you can make a go of it," I replied. "London, New York, LA, and Nashville, there aren't many. It takes a lot of money to get started in New York and London, and the market is saturated in LA. That leaves Nashville, and Nashville is just starting to boom since country music went pop. Nashville artists are actually touring big now."

"Do you think you can make it in Nashville?"

"Yes," I said, "absolutely. I just have to find a building."

"Good! Start looking," he said. "I'm your new partner."

A few days later, I was on a plane to Nashville. Then a local Nashville banker said without blinking, "OK, you want to build it here, no problem, how much do you need?" And just like that, we had a loan using Glenn's assets to open the door, and we became fifty-fifty partners in our new endeavor. It didn't take long to come up with a name. It just sort of rolled off Glenn's tongue, "Sound Check." It was perfect.

From day one, Glenn enjoyed being partners in Soundcheck. He even had his wife's birthday party in one of our studios. Most importantly, Glenn trusted me. He knew I wasn't going to screw him. We remained partners for the whole time I had the place.

We used Glenn's bookkeepers in LA. It was great because we got excellent financial management from them and all the free advice I could ever need. In the beginning, when we were still attracting a clientele, I called the accountant Barry. "Barry, I'm broke, I don't have a nickel."

"What's wrong," he said.

"I don't have any money."

"What are you doing about it?"

"Nothing," I said, "we just don't have any money."

"OK," "I'm gonna tell you what not to do,"

"What not to do?"

"Stop writing checks," was his answer and solution.

"OK, I can do that," I said.

"Give yourself two weeks," Barry said, "Stop writing checks for two weeks, and you'll be OK."

I had been at my wit's end, and Barry came through with a simple solution.

One time previously, when we needed a cash infusion, I called Glenn. Hat in hand, I said, "Glenn, we're gonna need some cash."

"How much do you want?" He replied.

"About a hundred thousand," I said.

Glenn replied simply, "Call Barry."

So, I called Barry.

"Barry, I just talked to Glenn. He said to give me a hundred thousand."

His gruff and terse answer was. "You did not!"

"I'll hold on this line," I said. "You use one of your twelve lines and give Glenn a call."

But Barry was outstanding. He was a typical accountant business manager, gruff and angry talk, just to keep me in line. Occasionally he'd get me on the phone and say, "What the hell are you spending money on now?"

At Soundcheck, we didn't start making money right off the bat. Our very first big client was Marty Stuart. In the last days of the old twangy Nashville paradigm, Marty had been ahead of the curve doing a hipper, more modern version of country. He spotted our worth in the community and began using us almost immediately.

Our second client was a country star, John Berry. ("Don't think I ain't a country 'cos I don't drive a big truck… Don't think I ain't country 'cos I ain't down on my luck")

Next was the great female country music, TV, and film star, Reba McIntire.

One day Reba's production manager walked in the front door out of the blue. He introduced himself, explaining that he was looking for a studio for Reba to rehearse in. "Do you have one we can rent?"

I said, "Sure, I've got four studio's you can rent, take your pick." We walked around and looked at the options, and when he made his choice, I said, "You got it, when do you want to start?" He answered, "The Trucks are in the parking lot."

His was a familiar story. Like Tina Turner at Third Encore, they had a place secured, but it was canceled out by the owners at the last minute.

As it turned out, having Reba come in was a great endorsement of our facilities and our family-friendly atmosphere, and excellent services. Reba had the luxury of a brand-new studio at her disposal, with brand new equipment, and her production manager was a hero for making lemonade out of lemons. For

Toni and me, history had repeated itself in Nashville, and once again, it worked in our favor.

Reba became the first Queen of Soundcheck. Whatever she or her staff and crew wanted or needed, we got it for them promptly. Unlike other rehearsal facilities, we did things with energy and enthusiasm. Before long, that would become our stock in trade.

It was the beginning of our long service-oriented history at Soundcheck. We became a who's who of top country artists and the place to be if you were a musician in a band.

But Long before the word got out and the first artist came through our door, Soundcheck began as a construction project.

We were great with the business, equipment, customer service, and the unique entertainment and entertainer aspects. Still, we'd have a lot to learn about local politics and local building codes that, in many ways, were 180 degrees from LA. Even before that, we'd have to educate and enlighten the powers that be at city hall as to what it actually was that we intended to build. They had no clue. It was up to us to get the concept across. Some of them were still fighting a war that happened in the mid-1800s. Having a Yankee New Jersey accent and a high energy level didn't help.

And that's where the story of Soundcheck really begins.

22

If You Build It They Will Come

After I sold Third Encore, I really missed it. I wasn't quite depressed about it, but I really missed what I had built there. Then when Glenn got involved, I became energized again. I was jazzed and looking forward to the new challenge and taking the new enterprise a step farther into the future.

I began commuting back and forth to Nashville, looking for a building. It took me about nine months to find a suitable place, the old AT&T building on Cowan Street, on the banks of the Cumberland River.

When it came time to finance the enterprise, Barry, Glenn's business manager, came in, and we went to three banks to shop a loan. Glenn and I put in an equal amount of cash and became 50-50 partners. With Barry's help and using Glenn's name, we secured a loan for the balance to build the facility.

Once the loan was secured, we brought in Lonnie, our old contractor from Third Encore, to build Soundcheck because he had prior experience. In building Third Encore, Lonnie had gained valuable experience in the pitfalls of building that type of facility.

Meanwhile, Toni stayed behind in California, and I began looking for a rental house so Toni and Summer could join me. At that time, there was a severe lack of rental properties available in Nashville. I found just two places listed and immediately went to see them. I liked the one in Goodlettsville, just north of the city, a short commute from the facility. It was a four-bedroom home in a nice neighborhood of professional, educated people on a cul-de-sac that I thought would be perfect for us.

Toni and I usually made all those kinds of decisions together, so I told the owner that I'd have to call her in California then get back to him. He said, "If you have to clear it with your wife, this property will be gone by the time you get back to me." There really were no rentals in the area, and what few came along were snatched up immediately. That left me only one choice, and I rented it right on the spot, then called Toni to let her know.

Toni:

"Bobby called from Nashville and said, 'Guess what, we have a house.' I thought, 'OK, I better get packing,' and I did. Thank God my nephew Timmy Mustard was around. We had practically raised him. He is now an architect in LA."

"Then Summer and I headed down to Nashville. It was a bit of a shock after living in LA. Everything was green and lush, sort of like the Midwest, where I grew up. I was cozy with it. It was like the Midwest but with a Hillbilly faction. We became familiar with that syndrome during construction when they walked off the job on Friday's at 2pm saying, 'It's Friday, two o'clock. Beer time. We're outta here!'"

"We moved in March when Summer was a freshman in high school. I had to figure out what I was going to do with her. I didn't want to put her in school for just the last six weeks. Bobby was having the house painted when we got there, so we moved into a hotel for a while. By the time we got to the house, it was all nice and fresh for Summer and me. Meanwhile, Timmy stayed behind and packed up our house in Palmdale. We had rented that house to our neighbors three doors down and got totally burned on the deal. Once we got out of state, they stopped paying rent. With all our expenses for moving and living in Nashville, it was just too much for us, and we gave the Palmdale house back to the bank."

"A friend of ours with a company called People Movers moved our belongings and my Ford Explorer across the country in the same truck. Lonnie, our framer that had done Third Encore, apart from being the best framer in the world, was also a great mechanic. Lonnie and his friend loaded all their tools in Bobby's old Chevy pick-up and drove it to Nashville with no worries about breakdowns. Summer and I and our two little terriers Rosie and Lucy, lived in the hotel room until the truck arrived with our belongings. We all arrived in Nashville in pieces and bits."

With the family, our belongings, and the framers all in Nashville, we began building the facility. Our first challenge came up pretty quickly when we started to demolish the old office area. We were informed by the building inspector that it contained asbestos. By the current law, it had to be removed before any construction could begin. This was not disclosed to us when we made the deal for the property, and we hadn't planned on that expense. The asbestos had to be removed by a certified asbestos removal company. They showed up in their spacemen outfits to handle it. "It can't go to a regular landfill, either." They take it somewhere, a disposal site that is also certified. We learned that when you remove asbestos, you still own it. In fact, you own it for life. If that asbestos ever turns up again, you are legally responsible for it.

We planned to put lockers between all the rooms to keep the bleeding down between rooms. It was a lesson we learned the hard way from our experience at Third Encore in LA. But There was no building code in Nashville specifically for a Rehearsal Facility.

When I took the plans to the city to issue the building permits, the old codger behind the desk said, "What are you building here, a theater?" I said, "No, it's a rehearsal facility. "A dance hall?" he asked. "No, it's a rehearsal facility. A place where artists come to rehearse their shows before they take them on the road or into a recording studio." "Is it a dance hall?" I went several rounds with this hardheaded old so and so until he began to get on my nerves. "NO… it's… a… REHEARSAL…STUDIO…" I repeated slowly and deliberately. "A place for entertainers to rehearse… to practice. Then I spelled it out even further. "OK," I said, "picture this, Garth Brooks is going on tour," (I thought maybe a country music reference might help) "he needs to practice his show before he plays to the public, so Garth rents a room from us where he and his band can practice before they go out on tour." Nothing… No response… I had drawn a blank again.

I imagined visions scrolling through his mind of an old 1940s movie theater with an ornate ticket booth and ushers dressed like bellhops, leading people to their seats. The image alternated with scenes of a ten cent a dance joint where complacent young women lined the sidelines, standing-by to take customers for a spin across the dance floor, under a brightly lit mirror ball.

The old codger about wore me out. He had no inkling or the imagination to remotely, possibly, even get a clue as to what I was talking about. He was from so far out in the country that the sun went down between his house and town.

I never did get through to him. Being a Yankee with a New Jersey accent, and in their eyes, a carpetbagger didn't help either. It just made a bad situation worse. Eventually, the old codger threw up his hands, so to speak, and took it to his superiors. They determined that the local building commission would have to review the situation and make a ruling. Fine with me, as long as it kept things moving in the right direction. But I was adamant as well. I wanted the plans to be labeled *"Rehearsal Facility,"* not theater... not dance hall... not barn, or chicken coop... "rehearsal facility."

In the meantime, our hands were tied. We couldn't as much as hammer in a nail until the commission decided because no one knew what building codes applied; therefore, no one knew what standards to apply to our construction. This involved even more politics. We had to go to the planning commission meetings to get them to put us on their agenda to determine the codes that would apply to us.

Once the commission was satisfied, another curveball came at us. This time they would not allow Lonnie, our contractor, the guy with the experience that built Third Encore, to work without a Tennessee contractor's license. We had to hire a local contractor to act as our frontman. All labor and materials purchase payments went through the contractor, and Lonnie and all the tradesmen would be paid by him. We didn't like that, and we had no choice, but at least construction began.

Toni:

Finally, everything seemed to have settled down, and at last, work began. "We had to pay the local contractor/frontman ten thousand dollars upfront. Also, every time we ordered something, we had to pay the frontman, and he paid the suppliers."

"Bobby was back on the road with Glenn. I began getting phone calls from suppliers. They weren't getting paid."

In Nashville, the local contractors association has a weekly credit meeting to keep up on who in town is paying their bills and vice versa. We were about to be put on their blacklist, which would most likely have resulted in us getting cut off from building materials in town. And the good name we were hoping to build would have been ruined.

"But We were paying our frontman every time the materials were ordered, and he wasn't paying the suppliers. I called Bobby on the road immediately."

"Bobby went to Glenn and said, I have to get out of here, I have to fly back to Nashville and straighten this thing out."

I came into town on a Friday. We were about $29K in debt with the suppliers, but we had already paid the frontman that money. It was his responsibility to pay the suppliers on time from the money we had already given him. Then we set a meeting with the frontman, luring him in with the promise of his next payment.

When he arrived, Toni quietly escorted him into studio "A." He thought he was there to get his next payment. But I was waiting inside. As soon as the studio door closed and Toni exited the room, I flashed a pistol at the guy and told him flat out that if the suppliers weren't paid by Monday morning, he was going to end up in the Cumberland River with cement shoes on. He was clearly a shyster. I had met him on his home turf and scared the crap out of him.

"We had clearly set him up, but that's how you had to do business with him. If we Hadn't forced the issue, we would have ended up his victim. Unfortunate, but it had to be done. It had to get ugly before it could get better."

Thank God we had Lonnie, our LA contractor. It was he who tipped us off. He was an honest guy. The other construction workers and the suppliers confided in him as one of their own, and he told Toni.

Promptly Monday morning, the frontman showed up with a check for the $29K we owed the vendors. Toni immediately deposited it in our account and this time, forget the rules, she paid off the vendors herself and explained to them and the contractor's association what had happened. From then on, all we used him for was to sign for the permits and anything else that required a contractor's signature. It had all worked out well. It put Lonnie, our LA guy, back in charge of construction where he should have been from the start and eliminated the frontman. It also put Toni back where she belonged, in control of the money.

After that, it was pretty smooth sailing. The city required that we use aluminum drywall studs. In LA, we used wood. But even if we could have used wood, they just didn't make twenty-six-foot lengths of two by fours. That was how high our ceilings went, but below that was a grid that ended up at about 24 feet.

Lonnie dealt with the subcontractors and did all the framing. The framing was just a matter of shooting the metal studs into the concrete floor and plumbing them up. It was a simple process.

The drywall contractor was a good guy. He ended up being a good friend of mine. Per the code, he installed a layer of Drywall, a soundboard layer, and so forth about thirteen inches thick. Despite the slow and casual southern work ethic in Nashville, everything turned out OK.

Every time a significant task like plumbing, electrical, or framing, from any of the crafts, was started or completed, or when a room was completed, the city inspector showed up. Our inspector turned out to be a guy named Sonny, a Giant of a man at about six feet nine inches tall.

I met with him the first day and had to look up to see his face. We walked the building together, and I mentioned the two exits in each room. Then he pointed out that one of the exterior doors had no access as a fire escape. That would require us to create a hallway between two of the studios. It hadn't been drawn in on the plans, and the city completely missed it when they OK'd the plans.

I did some quick figuring and came up with a number. It would cost us another ten thousand dollars to build an egress between the rooms to create the required fire exit. It wasn't going to be usable space, and we couldn't rent it out, but we did see the logic from a safety point of view. We called it the million-dollar hallway. Eventually, we kept pianos, organs, other keyboards, and the like against the walls and were still in compliance.

The city had passed the plans without the egress, the inspector caught the mistake, and we had to pay for it. Welcome to the world of construction… the good 'ole boy world of construction.

We removed a spiral staircase that had been in the old office area of the building. It looked like new and had cost someone quite a bit of money when it was new. Sonny, the building inspector, spotted it in a junk pile in the back of the building. He was hinting that he wanted it, most likely for its scrap or resale value, by asking what we were going to do with it.

"I was saving it for you," I said Facetiously,

"Yeah, I need it," he replied.

Toni:

"We decided we needed nice new linoleum at the entranceway that looked good and was durable enough that carts and cases could roll over it. It was going to cost about eight thousand dollars, but we were running short of money. Bobby was on the road with Glenn. He had to ask Glenn to sign a note for a loan to buy $8K worth of linoleum for Soundcheck that we'd payback, but we needed to use Glenn's name."

We had bought the house we were renting, and I thought the linoleum we pulled out of Soundcheck would look good in our kitchen. The next time Sonny came by, he saw the linoleum and hinted in his not so subtle way, "I like that linoleum. That would look good in my daughter's house" "So do I," I said. "I'm going to take it home and put it in the kitchen." Then Bobby said, "Uh, Toni… No, you're not." He ended up giving the linoleum to Sonny.

"Hey, whatever it takes, Bobby said."

Sonny was a real piece of work. I'm sure he was making a tidy little sum on our discards. "We bought all new toilets and sinks and fixtures for the restrooms. He took all the old ones. He took them all. He took everything."

What did I get for it? His sign off on the inspections. I needed a friend, and he was a friend... he signed off, and we had no more problems.

Toni:

"Bobby was back on the road again with Glenn and Joe Walsh. We called it *The Glenn And Joe Tour*. Now I'm in charge of everything."

By then, the walls were all finally up, and we installed 5-ton air conditioners for each studio that regulated the temperature in each room individually.

Summer and I went to work there first thing every morning. Summer was about thirteen years old in her freshman year of High School. She was a good little camper. We had told her what we were going to do, and she was supportive. She was like, "Whatever mom and dad want to do."

Everything was going well, that is, until Sonny showed up with the Fire Marshall. They looked at our walls that had finished out at about 24 feet and decided that we had to caulk them all the way to the ceiling. Their reasoning was that it would prevent the flames from jumping from room to room in case of fire.

We thought it was overkill, and they may have still been evaluating us using the codes that relate to a multiplex theatre.

All I heard was Cha-Ching! The sound of a cash register being rung up again. It turned out to be another costly revelation at 500 dollars a bucket for the mud. But it was fireproof mud, and it was our mud.

We found a contractor that specialized in that type of caulking, Gary Faulkner. He came in and erected 24-foot-high scaffolding to work from. Gary turned out to be a wonderful person, and we became friends with him.

Bobby said of Soundcheck at that point that it was like holding up a bank. But by then, we were at the point of no return, and the end was finally in sight.

We didn't have the best electrical plan because I knew nothing about electrical at that time, and Lonnie didn't know electrical either. We only put 100 amps in each room, which was not enough for modern theatrical equipment when you have lighting and sound and video equipment all going at the same time.

Then, by the end of November, we finally got our occupancy permit.

And no one came.

23

Then, They Came…

It was a glorious day, that day in November, when we got our occupancy permit. The Angels were singing. It had been almost nine months since the project was conceived in March. It was our baby, and we carried it to term. The great ordeal of building Soundcheck was finally over. Now, at last, we could carry on with our trade.

We went to every recording studio in town and put up our business card. Glenn was supposed to come down for the opening party with his band, so we sent out about 300 invitations to anyone and everyone we could think of, including management companies.

At that point, no one in town gave a damn about us. If we had a hundred people at our party, we were lucky. And honestly, many of them were the construction crews and their families.

Glenn had offered to bring his band down to play at the opening party. But a few days before the party, Glenn got sick. He called to let us know that he couldn't make it, but he had a plan B. "I'm sending everybody down," he said. "I'm paying for the band, round trip flights, and a hotel, the whole works, and I'll get Joe to replace me. Don't worry, I'll fix it with Joe."

We met Joe at the airport. He had a girlfriend with him, and they were both loaded for bear. We made nice with Joe and thanked him for coming. His response was that he needed to party a bit before he went on stage. We were delegated to get him there. "You want me to play," he said, "I have to feel good before I play." We had no idea of how we were going to make that happen, but eventually, someone helped us locate some of the Peruvian marching powder Joe favored, and once he felt good, he got on stage. He did a good set with Glenn's guys, "The Heaters," the band from the Glenn and Joe tour, and everyone enjoyed it. But what's not to like... It was, after all, Joe Walsh, doing his thing. It was Joe being Joe. Thank God he didn't ask for a chain saw.

The word of Joe's appearance had partially gotten out amongst a few players in town. Despite the low numbers at the party, everyone was having a good time. Vince Gill and Steve Wariner had both shown up, along with a bunch of other players. When Joe walked in, the word was chanted in whispers like a mantra, and it spread around the room. "Joe's messed up... Joe's messed up!"

Most Nashville artists didn't get the concept of a dedicated rehearsal facility. They were still rehearsing in their busses and at the venue on their first tour date. Garth Brooks was one of the first Nashville artists to tour with full production. But Garth had his own rehearsal spot.

People that came in to see the studios would say, "Why did you build these rooms so big?" I'd answer, "For touring productions. Now Nashville artists can rehearse with the lighting and all the gear they take on tour. Most would look at me with quizzical looks on their faces."

One tour manager that came in to check us out said, "You should have free peanuts and let people throw the shells on the floor, so it feels more like home." We thought, "What do we look like, a local tavern?" He would have been the first person to gripe when his band's road cases wouldn't roll over peanut shells. It was a hugely lame idea! Nobody said you had to be a Mensa member to be a tour manager. Maybe he lived like that in his house, but in ours, we were all about service and taking care of our customers.

There were two other rehearsal complexes in Nashville. One was big in LA in equipment rentals and rehearsal halls and built a few small rooms adjacent to their equipment rental facility in Nashville. But they were no way on par with what we had done at Third Encore and what we had built at Soundcheck.

The owner was someone everyone in the LA music community knew of. He came in one day to scope out the competition. I saw him lurking around at the end of the hallway and checking things out. I introduced myself to him and welcomed him to Soundcheck. He had come in with a war mentality and made it abundantly clear that there was not room enough in Nashville for the two of us. "I'm your competition," he said. I quickly replied, "Competition is good; it keeps you on your toes."

The other rehearsal facility was a "down-home" type place. It had a few dingy little studios. Its owner also paid Soundcheck a visit with nearly the same attitude as the last guy. He also showed up with his war face on.

There is a prevailing theory in Nashville that everything goes in eight-year cycles. Trends peak high and dip low. During the lows, new trends are established, and the cycle begins to climb again. Like a factory, Nashville retools between trends. We had apparently arrived at the low point of the process. We had nowhere to go but up.

John Berry was a great guy, a great singer, a well-respected artist in the industry, and our first client. John rehearsed at Soundcheck for about 3 days. Unfortunately, John's career lasted about a minute and a half. But he was our first, and we will always be grateful for that. John was the perfect introduction to Nashville's music community when our very existence was in question in our minds.

Shortly after John, Marty Stuart came in. Marty had played guitar for Johnny Cash when some country musicians courted the idea of heavier beats, hipper vocals, and meaty guitars and solo's, thanks no doubt to bands like Poco and The Eagles. But in those days, Nashville did not embrace rapid changes and moved into the future at a snail's pace. When that time finally came, Marty Stuart was one of the leaders. He played on landmark projects of his own, as well as The Highwaymen with Johnny Cash, Kris Kristofferson, Waylon Jennings, and Willy Nelson. Marty had been sort of a bridge to the future, embracing traditional music as well as the newer trends in his era.

Marty loved Soundcheck. He was a pretty friendly guy that always wore cowboy shirts and great boots. Like most musicians, Marty was a unique individual. In Nashville, one story has Marty shopping at Walmart at 3am when the store wasn't crowded to avoid his fans' usual onslaught.

Marty came in one cold, snowy morning wearing a pair of Uggs instead of cowboy boots. They made them for men and women, and I fell in love with them. I complimented him on his choice of footwear. At that time, they were wildly popular among teenage girls. They wore them with a variety of outfits. After that, I had to have a pair of men's Uggs for myself.

When Vince Gil discovered us, he asked to see a locker, so I showed him a few. He liked one of our bigger ones. It would have held three times the equipment he was going to put in it. "Honestly," I said, "this is more room than you need. Are you sure it's what you want? It costs a little more than most of the others."

"Nope, I don't care about the cost," he said.

His crew must have loved him for it since it was close to the loading dock. After a long road tour, it would only take them a short time to get their gear out of the truck and into the locker. They could be home at rest in no time flat.

The word was getting out about Soundcheck in Nashville.

Artists that had never considered it before began to use our facilities. Many rented lockers from us as well. Lockers were a mainstay of our business. A band or single artist could rent a locker to keep their gear in for a reasonable fee. When they booked a room, we would help them load-in and set-up. We'd provide them with a PA system, mics, and a comfortable place to sit between sessions. If they had a locker, they were only steps away from any additional equipment they might need from their own inventory. On top of that, we had some of the top vendors, sound companies, microphone manufacturers, keyboards, and a drum shop on site.

Other rehearsal halls in town were sort of mom and pop and didn't provide near the level of facilities and services that we, as veterans of many road tours with top bands, could offer. We looked at our road experience as a big plus. When you're on the road with a show, you eat, drink, and think about taking care of the musicians, their gear, and the show, twenty-four hours seven days a week, rain or shine, sleep or no sleep. We brought the concept of a top-notch full-service rehearsal hall to Nashville.

We'd also had a great staff at 3E. We even had one kid with no road experience that really stood out. He wanted to be a sound engineer. It was his passion. He worked the late shift for us, tearing down band gear and the sound system, coiling cables, and packing up microphones. He'd sometimes stay there all-night practicing on our sound equipment. He ended up taking a road gig with an artist that was popular at that time called Bruno Mars. I have no doubt that he went on to bigger and better things.

Reba McIntyre was a mainstream country superstar with many hit records, TV, and movie credits under her belt. Reba was our third client. She has the second-most wins for the Academy of Country Music's Top Female Vocalist Award. The story goes that she almost did not make it on her debut night at the Grand Ole Opry because her name was accidentally overlooked when she checked in at the stage door.

After Reba came in, the entire music community began knocking on our door for rehearsal space and locker rentals. Then after Reba, a string of female artists began to use us. Besides the facility itself, I think initially it had to do with them feeling safe and well cared for.

Tanya Tucker was the third female to use us regularly. She and her group were pleasant enough to deal with, and she was a real fun-loving gal. In her career, she identified with the Outlaw genre. On CMT's Dozen Greatest Outlaws list, she was ranked number nine.

Dolly Parton, another of our earliest clients, rehearsed at Soundcheck often. Toni loved Dolly.

Toni:

"Dolly was the most beautiful woman I have ever seen. When she came into the office, I was completely stunned by her beauty. She's not only beautiful, but she has the best smelling perfume. Dolly was down to earth as well. She hung out in the lounge, teasing back and forth with her guys and having fun."

When Dolly was in, I could follow the trail of her perfume wherever she was. It was intoxicating. One day we got a call in the office for Dolly from a backup singer. She wanted me to let Dolly know she was going to be late for rehearsal. I found Dolly and gave her the news. In her trademark cutesy drawl, she said sarcastically, "I swear, that girl is always late."

Barbara Mandrell was one of the hardest working women I've ever seen in the industry. She booked a studio at Soundcheck for three months. She'd show up at 9am, and our dog Sophie, a Blue Tick Heeler, would be waiting for her at the door.

Blue Heelers are an Australian breed. We rescued her outside of Soundcheck when she was just a puppy. As cattle and sheepherders, they are highly active working dogs. Good looking and smart. Their instinct is to nip at the heel of stragglers to get them back in the herd. They are loyal and often form bonds with the people they work for and the people who take them as pets.

Sophie had adopted Barbara to look after, and vice versa. Barbara loved Sophie, and the feeling was mutual.

Each morning Barbara arrived promptly at 9am with a rawhide pig ear for Sophie, who was dutifully waiting for her arrival. Sophie walked her the entire way to the rehearsal studio then returned to her spot to eat her pig ear.

Toni:

"Barbara was a warm person that seemed to have been through a lot. I thought she always had a need to explain herself. Barbara had only been with us for a couple of days when she came into the office, where we had one of Glenn's nice turquoise leather art-deco couches. She introduced herself and sat down for a chat. She wanted us to know that she really appreciated Soundcheck and what we did for her. She was wearing a seven and a half-carat diamond ring. I noticed it right off but didn't say a word. That would have been rude."

"But She made a point of showing me the ring and letting me know how big it was, but she also said, 'I've earned every penny for this ring.' She wanted us to know she wasn't trying to show off; she just enjoyed nice things. Barbara just wanted us to accept her. They routinely broke for lunch between 12pm and 1pm then went right back to work. She frequently had lunch catered in, and Bobby and I were always welcome to partake".

Toni:
 Sophie was the best friend anyone could ever ask for.

"When we were building Soundcheck, Bobby was frequently out of town with Glenn Frey. A few times, the alarm went off in the middle of the night. I'd call the police, and Sophie and I would jump in the car and go down to check it out. The cops met us there. Then once I opened the door, the cops left, and Sophie and I would be on our own. I'd say, wait a minute, what if someone is in the building? The cops left us there alone, saying they had other calls. Then Sophie and I walked the building by ourselves with no gun, no weapons, peeking behind curtains, and everywhere. Protect and serve…right! Sophie was the only one doing any serving or protecting."

Barbara Mandrell was Sophies' favorite person at Soundcheck, and mostly everyone loved Sophie as well. Winona Judd was a big fan of hers and also formed a close bond with Sophie. She was just a lovable little dog, bred to have a sense of duty toward the people she loved.

Randy Travis, however, was allergic to dogs. Randy's road manager would call to book a week for Randy with one condition, "Sophie Can't be there." We respected that, and Sophie had to sit it out at home alone for the week.

Randy kept to himself during his time at Soundcheck. He wasn't very social, and we didn't have much contact with him.

Johnny, the lead singer of Lynyrd Skynyrd, became Toni's friend. Johnny wasn't a dog person, and he didn't like having many people around him. One day he came out to our "lobby" for a break. It was a nice comfortable little area with a couch and chairs where clients could get away from their work for a quiet moment. We always put out a bowl of Jolly Ranchers hard candy. When Johnny sat down on the couch, Sophie jumped up next to him. Then Johnny, the guy who didn't like dogs, began petting her. Johnny fell in love with Sophie. Soon, he started spending more time on the couch with Sophie than he did rehearsing with the band. Everyone loved Sophie.

Toni remembers the first time Clint Black came in:

"I have a habit of shaking hands. But unless Clint knows you, Clint can be a bit germophobic, so he wouldn't shake my hand. But Clint ended up being a great guy and one of our best clients. He was there frequently, and he absolutely loved Sophie. Sometimes we'd get calls from the staff at 8pm to say, 'Clint Black is down here playing basketball.'"

A close friend who tour managed an all-female group, *The Pointer Sisters,* told me a funny story he'd heard Clint tell. He took the group to a photoshoot regarding a show they were mutually booked on with Clint to welcome home troops from Operation Desert Storm. Clint told the *Sisters* a family of African Americans called the White's lived in the neighborhood he grew up in. They were known as the black Whites, and Clint's family were known as the white blacks.

Soundcheck was a place where entertainers could rehearse, and no one knew they were there. We never advertised to the public. Everything was word of mouth, and that kept it private, a place where everyone could be themselves.

Toni:

"Steven Curtis Chapman was a popular Christian artist. Steven was a huge star in Christian music. He was a family man. He and his wife even adopted a bunch of kids. We had a basketball court that just about everyone that came in played on. At times Steven wore a whistle on a lanyard around his neck and a referee's shirt. He was dead serious about basketball. He brought his kids in, and they roller-skated all over Soundcheck. (Summer also Roller skated around to open up lockers in the far corners of the building.) When Steven came in with the kids, we'd let them roller skate around and do what they wanted. Steven knew where they were and knew they were safe. We made Soundcheck a safe environment for all the kids. The big kids rented the studios to play and rehearse music in and brought their children in to play as well."

Steve Wariner was a hugely popular country artist that charted more than fifty singles and countless albums on the Billboard country charts. Steve was a trip, one of the most fantastic guys in the world. He and his band chose up sides and played basketball against each other. One day I joked, "Steve, you know you gotta sometimes rehearse too. Give someone else a chance to play ball." Steve laughed.

Summer worked with us at Soundcheck as well. She was pregnant when Peter Frampton asked her if she had any weed. She answered, "Are you kidding? My dad would kill me if I brought weed in here. No, I don't have any weed, and I can't get any either." A downside of being part of Soundcheck was that people from the music community looked after Summer if she was out on the town or at a party. They'd remind her to behave herself. Back then, the music community in Nashville was a small and tight-knit bunch of folks that looked after each other. Because she was our daughter, Summer could get into any concert or party around town. There was always someone there that said, "You're Norton's daughter, we have our eye on you!" She could never party too much for fear of it getting back to Toni and me.

Toni and I always drove separately to work. Toni liked having her car to go to the bank, do her errands on her own, and have transport if anything happened to Summer at school.

Toni:
"I was the one that opened up. I'm an early riser. I'd get there at seven each morning, walk through all the rooms to be sure they were clean and tidy, and if need be, clean them myself. Bobby

217

would get in around 9am when the clients arrived. I tried to get out by about 5:30 or 6pm to get home to be a mom. Bobby would come home about a half-hour later.

We had a good routine. Bobby had his clients, and I had my clients."

One day a familiar face walked through our door. It was Walter Egan. Walter was one of the first artists I'd ever toured with. He was the guy with the wild backup singer that I'd have to coax out of her room and into transportation every morning on the road. Walter had always been pleasant to work for, but when he walked into Soundcheck that morning, he was flat broke.

Walter heard from someone in Nashville that I had become successful with Soundcheck and stopped in to ask a favor. It wasn't a huge favor, but it spoke volumes of his current situation. We talked for a few minutes then he finally got around to the favor. "Can you lend me twenty dollars? I'm trying to get a teaching job, and I'm tapped out at present."

It took me a few seconds to realize that he was on the up and up and to see how desperate he had become. Without hesitation, I gave him the money. It was sad. He used to pay my salary, and now I was lending him twenty dollars just to get by on.

Eventually, as time went on, he landed a teaching job and made a point of paying back the money, all but one dollar. Today I occasionally run into Walter. The private joke between us is that he still owes me a dollar.

Another of the string of female Country artists that began using our services was Faith Hill. Toni and I both enjoyed having her at Soundcheck because she was so wonderful to work with. Faith was just a beautiful person.

During the time she was rehearsing with us, she lost a diamond and had no idea where. We didn't know if it was lying on the studio floor, at her house, or if her dog ate it. We put together a search party and searched every inch of every studio and every corner of the facility, over one hundred thousand square feet of space, looking for that diamond to no avail.

Then Winona Judd, Leanne Rimes, and Trisha Yearwood each came in at separate times. They all became pals with Sophie as well.

Sophie was building a growing fan base amongst our clients.

At the time, John Fogerty and his band, Credence Clearwater Revival, had been the first artists to accept a booking for the original Woodstock Festival. John Fogerty opened the door, and all the others became involved because of him. In a recent interview, he talked about how he was unhappy with the slot they had given Credence since Credence was instrumental in many other artists getting on board.

Toni:
"John Fogerty and his brother Bob came into Soundcheck. Bob was a good guy. Bob took care of everything for John, including all his personal equipment, and was even more

personable than John. John was a Nice guy and friendly, but Bob was more outgoing."

"We would be in the office, and every time the studio door opened, I heard one of his songs bleed out of the room. I was amazed. I'd look at Bobby and say, 'He did that one too? His catalog is unbelievable.'"

John Also had an incredible and rare amplifier collection.

"Toni is absolutely right. Fogerty's brother Bob and I were talking one day about vintage Fender amplifiers. He said, 'You want to see some vintage fender amps? Come with me.' We went to their locker, Bob unlocked it, and my mind was blown. He had what I estimated to be one of almost every amplifier Fender ever made in the company's history. John had big ones, little ones, all the popular models, and many I had never seen before. Then he showed me John's guitar collection. He had more guitars than the entire Eagles band combined, and we had over 40 guitars on that show."

Whenever an artist came into Soundcheck, I walked them to their room. I liked John a lot, I thought he was a great guy. One day John made a stop at his locker. I said, "John, this is the best collection of amps and guitars I've ever seen." He said, "It took me a long time... a long time."

Alan Jackson also rehearsed at Sound Check, and I liked him a lot as well. But I gained even more respect for him after he stood up for George Jones, considered the greatest singer in the history of Country Music.

The CMA awards wouldn't allow George Jones to sing his nominated hit in its entirety on the show. They wanted him to just sing a verse and chorus. Everybody knows that country music is a genre that respects its elders, and George Jones, despite the personal demons he wrestled with for a time, was one of its elder statesmen. That didn't sit well with George, so he decided not to do the show at all.

It upset Alan Jackson, a country superstar and a friend of Jones. After Jackson sang his current hit, he abruptly launched into a chorus of Jones' song "Choices." When he finished, Jackson walked off the show as a protest to the way the CMA handled the situation with George Jones. The next day the entire music business was buzzing about it, and many fans agreed with them.

When Alan came in after the show had aired, I said to him, "That was very cool what you did for George Jones." A man of few words, he replied, "Yeah, I was real happy."

One day a stranger came into Soundcheck. I introduced myself and asked how I could help him. "I have the entire remains of the Lynyrd Skynyrd, plane crash," He replied, "I was told to take them here, to Soundcheck."

I was a bit confused, "Wasn't that plane crash a few years ago? What would you like me to do with it?"

"They want you to store it, he said."

"OK, pick a locker," I answered.

He picked a locker, and I went up front, corralled two of my guys, and said, "Let's go, we have a terrible job to do." We took a couple of carts and headed to the loading dock. Just the thought of what we had to do next was gruesome.

The Lynyrd Skinner truck backed into the loading bay. When the door was opened, the stench was overwhelming. To put it mildly but plainly, it stunk to high heaven. It was a stench from hell, the stench of burned flesh, electronic equipment, textiles, plastics, jet fuel, and other unidentifiable odors. All in all, it looked and smelled like tragedy and heartbreak to me.

We had the remains of everything that had been on that plane when it went down, band gear, instruments, stage clothes, everything. We'd each take a cartload to the locker, drop it off, then head back for more, gagging all the while. It was a sooty, smelly, messy job, and for all the good it did, I gave my guys gloves and t-shirts to wear.

When the job was done, I asked the stranger that brought everything in with the truck, "Who do I bill for this?" He gave me a number and said, "Call this guy."

I called him immediately. He identified himself as one of the band's road managers. "I have the stuff you sent from Skynyrd's plane crash. What do I do with it?" "Just store it," he said. "By the way, what is the cost?" I gave him a number. "Just send us the bill," he said, "we'll pay it monthly."

A few months later, another stranger walked in with an attitude from here to Chicago. "Who owns this joint" he snapped.

"I do…" I answered, "and actually it's not a 'joint,' it's a rehearsal facility. The most prominent people in Country Music are our clients. …And who are you?" I offered my neck getting redder and redder every second. He bunched up his shoulders like he was going to make a move on me, and I said counseling caution, "Don't do it… Don't do it!"

He had come in both guns blazing, looking to pick a fight. I'd seen guys like him on low rent band crews my whole life. Everyone other than them is a "rube," therefore the object of subjugation. He was a low rent guy with an overstated sense of himself and his place in the grand scheme. Precisely the opposite of the Nashville entertainment scene where a common catchphrase was "don't get above your raising." In other words, treat people well and don't be arrogant and uppity.

He was sent to Nashville to look at the remains, evaluate what was left, and report it to the man paying the bills. But there was nothing left but burnt and tattered remnants of clothing, band gear, and personal effects, and I said so.

"I'm here to pay the bill," he finally offered with a bit of an edge to his voice.

"You're paying the bill for the storage? Are you taking it with you?"

"No," he answered.

"OK," I said, "It's been here for several months," you owe us for the rental. I could see the guy's attitude begin to flare up when I gave him the cost. He went off to make a phone call, and when he returned, he reluctantly agreed. I gave him the caveat that if the rent wasn't paid each month, I would move the contents into the dumpster. That set him off again. "Why are you such a prick?" He barked at me.

"I'm not a prick; I'm a businessman. We make our living here, renting rehearsal halls and lockers. Take it or leave it, your choice."

A few months later, he came back again and said, "We want to keep the locker. We'll keep it for three months." They kept it until long after I sold the place and the new owners took over. His belligerence would later prove to have been futile.

Another twist to the story was that the reorganized Lynyrd Skynyrd, band began to rehearse with us as well, and the replacement lead singer found a new friend in Sophie.

Soundcheck had improved on our previous studios in LA in every possible way. We were Third Encore on Steroids, with a touch of class, and in many ways catering to a much better clientele. We also had several vendors with offices on site. Sound Image, a tremendous touring sound company, had an office, and it was really convenient to have Shure Microphones and wireless systems in-house as well.

Once Soundcheck was established, we were recognized as respected members in good standing of the tight-knit Music community in Nashville. Everyone in that community knew us or knew of us.

We provided friendly, courteous service in a family environment to all of our highly visible clients. I can honestly say that the artists felt safe and comfortable rehearsing in the environment we provided. They felt comfortable bringing their children with them. We had something for everyone, and the kids were safe and occupied with activities we provided like basketball, ping pong, and more.

We had become pillars of the community. Eventually, I joined an organization called Leadership Music, a not for profit organization that promoted camaraderie, communication, and dialogue among industry leaders, exposing them to varying points of view and philosophies.

At one of the Organization get-togethers, a familiar-looking guy introduced himself to me. I couldn't place his face until he said, "Are you, Norton?"

"Yes," I said, "my name is Bob Thompson, but they call me Norton."

"I'm Bernie Leadon," he responded. "I played guitar with the Eagles."

"Oh yeah," I said. "Good to meet you. You were there before my time."

From that moment on, we became very friendly with each other. We'd frequently team up when Leadership Music had some event or project that we could lend a hand on. We never told each other war stories, but we both knew there was a lot of common ground in what we *weren't* saying.

Toni and I had become good friends with Gary Faulkner, the man who did the mandated fireproof caulking at Soundcheck. I soon discovered that Gary had a love of baseball as did I. I'd played high school ball, and Gary asked if I'd help coach in the high school league he was involved in at Moss Right Park, adjacent to Goodlettsville Middle School and Hunters Lane High School. I started out with the high school kids, but later we coached the younger kids. One year we even won the championship series in Goodlettsville.

After about a year or two, I got involved with Dennis Birdwell, the baseball commissioner for the Goodlettsville town leagues, and we coached together. I did that for about seven years. When we won the division, we had to fly to Texas. I was able to get Garth Brooks to sponsor us. He paid for all the flights.

I called the team together and gave them a mandate for travel. As in professional baseball, everyone associated with the team was required to wear a white shirt, tie, khaki pants, and dress shoes.

These were not poor kids; in fact, most were the offspring of upper-middle-class professionals. When they griped about it, I laid down the law. "You want to make the trip, that's what you need. You're going to look like professionals, and you're going to act like it."

Although Garth Brooks paid the travel, the league had allocated money for per diems. Neither Dennis nor I wanted to have to dole out per diems, so we took Summer along to take care of per diems and generally help out as a sort of traveling secretary to the team. Summer loved it, she loves to be in charge, and she'd always done a great job at whatever she's taken on.

For a time, I became an assistant coach at Beech High School, another well-known school in the Nashville area, and ended up back with Dennis as an associate coach at Whitehouse Hermitage, where my coaching days ended.

Sadly, Dennis Birdwell passed away at the age of 45 in 2018. He was well respected as the man that coached two Little League World Series Teams from Goodlettsville.

After many years of Toni and me running Soundcheck and taking care of our clients, the day came when I grew tired of telling Eagles stories. Everybody wanted to hear an Eagles story. Not just that, but I became physically weary. I faced the fact that I was growing old. I had pondered this day briefly my entire life. But I had never dwelled on it. For most of my life and career, I had been bulletproof. Able to leap tall buildings in a single bound. I lived large, albeit in the shadow of giants. I'd seen much of the world at the expense of those giants. I gave counsel to the music heroes of our generation. I was "Norton." I was bigger than life, the guy everyone remembered. The guy they called when they needed things done, and recently the guy that had carved out a piece for himself in the history of the Rock n Roll, Touring, and Country Music industry in LA and in Nashville. I wasn't just somebody's guy anymore. I *was THE* guy, and Toni was the gal, and Soundcheck was well known and highly respected in the country music community. Even our dog Sophie had a high profile amongst our clients and was loved by all that met her.

At one point, half kidding, I blurted out how I felt. "I would sell this place to the first person that drops two bags of money on my desk."

It wasn't long before a man showed up at my door with just such an offer, and I accepted. After a bit of haggling back and forth, I got all I wanted from the sale. We sold off everything. The facility, all the fixtures, sound and lighting equipment, rental instruments, two trucks…everything!

While we still had Soundcheck, Toni and I had purchased a grand old house on ten acres, much of it on a hill at the base of a mountain. I bought a tractor with all the attachments to cut the grass and clear the brush. I busied myself with mowing, trimming trees, pruning, planting grass, and generally keeping the property spruced up and shipshape. I had several ATV's and all the tools and accouterments of the country gentleman I had become.

We left Soundcheck with more than enough money to see us through our golden years. Then, we sat back to watch the world rush by.

24

The Flood

How high's the water mama…

Four feet high and rising!

When Toni and I turned Soundcheck over to the new owner, it was with the understanding that he and his wife would run it as we had as a family business. Toni and I wanted our legacy to be preserved. We wanted the clientele we had built to continue to enjoy the same sort of personal family touch that we had been able to show them.

We were not unhappy with the deal that was made. On the contrary, we got everything we asked for. We were, however, disappointed that the new owner was more of a numbers guy. He was all about the bottom line. Toni and I had proven that we could make a handsome profit and still give the clients a quality experience. I'm not faulting the new owner, just saying.

Life was good in Goodlettsville, but Toni had another bout with cancer. Toni is a strong woman. She fought it hard, lived through the chemo, and came out on the other side as a two-time cancer survivor, yet still as active as ever. Today she keeps busy as a teacher's aide in the local school district.

Our daughter Summer graduated from college with a master's in education and teaches seventh and eighth graders in the local school district. She married and had a boy of her own, though sadly, she and her husband divorced. Their son splits his time equally between his parents and visits with us. We're very proud of our Grandson, always at the top of his class. He gets that from his mother and grandmother, two sharp cookies.

Even though I graduated from a Jesuit high school and had a few years of college, I'm not academic in the least. But I know people. I read them and win them over with my New Jersey charm and sense of humor. Mostly I trust my instincts and my sense of practicality.

Toni and I migrated from sunny Southern California, a couple of Yankees' in the prime of life, venturing forth in the land of country music to make our fortune. We were considered Yankee's for the first few years after we arrived in Nashville. We were able to prove ourselves in a land that was scarred by the likes of carpetbaggers and the shame of slavery and segregation and Jim Crow politics. But I have to say that most Nashvillians are warm and caring and industrious people that have long since risen above the stereotypes of past generations. Mainly I think, due to the influence the music has had on them. I believe having country music emanating from Nashville is a source of pride for most.

Toni and I are long past the level of "Yankee's." We settled here, became successful in business here, and our daughter graduated high school, and went on to college from here. We've risen to the level of "Damn Yankee's." The difference is that a Yankee comes to visit, a "Damn Yankee" takes up roots. We're proud to be Damn Yankee's from Nashville.

Nashville, the capital of Tennessee, was founded on the Cumberland River in the 1700s near Fort Nashborough. It was a strategic location as a river port for goods coming down the Cumberland from the Ohio River. Later in the 1800s, it became a railroad town and the first state capital to fall during the civil war.

Nashville has always been a river town and port. But in the twenty-first century, Nashville became the third fastest growing economy in the nation since the 1970s. In the 1980s, it bounced back from the Great Recession to become a top-five region for job growth.

Then, in 2010, the rains came.

All the forecasts predicted rain for Saturday, May 1, and Sunday, May 2, 2010. But when it came, it came in buckets. Huge buckets, cosmic sized buckets. Average rainfall was about 14 inches, 17 inches in places.

Saturday morning Old Hickory Lake, 25 miles upstream of the city, was resting peacefully at 444 feet above sea level. In the

1950s, the Cumberland River dam was built across the river in the town of Old Hickory as a significant "storage impoundment," creating Old Hickory Lake. I always took that to mean water for cities downstream was stored there, and when necessary, if the lake got too full, they released some of the water downstream to keep things in balance.

Old Hickory Lake is a popular recreational lake for camping and fishing, and recreational boating. The town of Hendersonville, on the lake, is dotted with the affluent homes of many of country music's greats.

Midday Saturday, the Corps Of Engineers head at the dam in the town of Old Hickory noticed that many of the streams and tributaries were beginning to swell. TV news showed a clip of a building floating down I-24. By then, everyone knew it was going to be bad. How bad? "Damn bad!" But no one knew just how "damn bad" bad could be. Eventually, it would exceed all expectations. The clincher has never been explained to my satisfaction. When and why were the floodgates opened at Old Hickory Dam, upriver from Nashville? I may never know.

By Sunday night, water was ripping through downtown Nashville. Gaylord Opryland resorts would eventually evacuate 1500 guests. Water was rapidly rising all over downtown Nashville. Emergency personnel had assured Opryland the water would not rise above the protective levees, but their own onsite security staff saw a more urgent situation. The water level at the Opry rose about 4 feet to the middle of the backstage door.

Soundcheck was four feet underwater. At Soundcheck, the new owners did not immediately act. They took a wait and see attitude and did nothing to protect the incredibly valuable heirloom musical instruments in costly storage lockers in their care. Perhaps they relied on the same emergency personnel that had initially informed Opryland.

But a marker pole near the river, clearly visible from Soundcheck, told a different story and forewarned disaster. The pole was a river gauge marked at intervals showing the current height of the river. Logically as the levels advanced, it should have rung alarm bells with the owners and prompted them to formulate an evacuation plan for the lockers. Had the pole been monitored, perhaps the advanced warning might have lessened the resulting loss and heartaches. Instead, no forethought was given, and no emergency plan was implemented. No warning phone calls were made to the owners of the priceless instruments stored at the facility; instruments musicians consider almost as appendages of themselves. Most were of significant historical, sentimental, and considerable monetary value. To many musicians, it was a travesty that showed a severe lack of respect and responsibility.

Sometimes a cash cow is not just a cow. Sometimes it's someone's pet as well. More often, it has been raised and nurtured from birth, sat up with nights, and lovingly cared for over many years. Sentimental? You bet it is.

Where musical instruments losses to the flood are concerned, some were not just priceless as tools of the trade; many were literally priceless ones of a kind, the journeyman tradesmen's investments for future retirement.

It's an age-old artist's dilemma. Artists, exceptionally sensitive people, are acutely aware of the beauty (or folly) of life. Should they expect others to feel so as well? Common sense should bridge that understanding, though common sense is a rare commodity. It takes frequent vacations. Even when it's at home, it is often ignored.

Opryland executives were acutely aware of the situation with the river. Right from the get-go, they communicated with each other and began to discuss the possibilities and plans of action. At around 6pm on Sunday, they sent senior staff members to assess the levees' potential to overflow. What they reported back up the chain was not good. The water was about 12 inches from overflowing.

Executives assembled guests in the Presidential Ballroom, the highest spot in the hotel, at 7pm to advise them of the situation. The water was 6 to 9 inches from the top of the levee.

The decision had been made by 8pm to evacuate the hotel and hundreds of employees. One executive said, "There was no hesitation. I didn't want a replay of New Orleans after Katrina."

By 8:15, the order was given to evacuate the theater. An effort to move precious Opry memorabilia and tapes to safety was also abandoned. Regardless, much was saved. A precious gun collection owned by Roy Acuff had been rescued by hotel executives.

By 9:30, the hotel evacuation had been completed. As a final measure, hotel security locked down the premises and swept each room to check for stragglers. They found one woman, oblivious of what was going on around her, fast asleep in her bed. Another guest was discovered hidden in a closet. She was hoping to avoid evacuation.

The entire hotel had been evacuated in short order, and guests were securely sheltered at McGavock High School, where senior executives brought the evacuees water, pizza, and doughnuts.

A few hours later, at about 1am, the floodwaters reached the front of the hotel. By 3am parts of the hotel had taken on 4 to 6 feet of water. The water at the backstage door of Opryland rose above the door handle, leaving only the Backstage door sign visible.

One Opryland executive commenting on the evacuation efforts said, "The most compelling override was to get our people and our customers out. We can't have any fatalities here. Buildings you can replace; people you can't."

Some five miles away as the crow flies, the owner of Soundcheck evacuated only his staff. He was later seen patrolling the grounds around the facility on a jet ski. This saddened me to no end. Though I had been away from the business for some time by then, I still had an emotional attachment to the place. More accurately, I was attached to the concept that I had conceived. My concept was based on years of caring for top musicians' instruments and realizing their value and what they meant to the human beings that played them.

Later, when the waters subsided, and the clean-up effort was underway, I saw a man, a top session player, leaving the facility crying over the loss of his precious instruments. Another top session player lost an irreplaceable guitar worth over $120K that was supposed to be his retirement. A major country music star, a loyal and longtime client of Soundcheck, lost the guitar his dad taught him on as a child. The stories go on and on.

The heart-rendering results of one country singer's tragedy were recorded on video and placed on YouTube titled: "Lorrie Morgan Soundcheck (after the flood)" by country singer Lorrie Morgan, then in the waning years of her career. I'd known Lorrie Morgan as the mother of one of the kids I coached in baseball.

The video's opening scenes are shot looking through the windshield of her car as she drives the recently opened road to Soundcheck to assess the damages on miscellaneous items and costumes she had in a storage locker.

The road to Soundcheck was a wet gash in the mountain of debris that lined the street on both sides, well above her car's height in spots. Inside the facility's main entrance, someone had set up a card table with a sign-in sheet and a Beware-of sign with the word "dog" covered over in white and the word "Snakes" in bold black letters and 3 exclamation points to emphasize the point.

Snakes, mud, and sewage from the river had spread

throughout the complex. The sign should also have warned of the health hazards the raw sewage posed to individuals handling their gear, and the community. Gloves were encouraged, and most customers and staff wore white filter face masks while in the facility.

The video shows Ms. Morgan at the door of her locker where the waterline at about 4 feet up the double door foretells the damages that await behind them. A sad and touching moment occurred when a helper hands her a plastic trash bag containing a sequined evening gown. Ms. Morgan reacted with deep emotion as she realized it was the soggy soiled remains of an expensive original Bob Mackie gown she wore on a memorable occasion at the peak of her career.

The camera pans to a water damaged electric guitar being pulled from the case, its neck and fretboard warped from being submerged in the polluted water. The entire backside of the acoustic guitar is pulled away from the body in sheets of laminate.

It is a horrific story experienced by countless others as they examined their priceless heirlooms. Some acoustic guitars were seemingly intact until they are removed from their cases and turned upside down. Murky water, sewage, and sludge pour out of the sound hole, the backsides warped and peeling.

Wooden instruments that in life rang out with music now lay in heaps and mounds piled up as Cumberland River holocaust victims one on top of the other. Twisted interwoven guitar bodies, necks protruding from the pile, are flood rendered as jetsam in primal sludge, haunted by the sounds that once poured forth from them in joyous rapture.

Musical instruments are not just material things. Many are handcrafted. Longed for in youth by passionate adolescents that spend minutes, hours, days and months, years; touching them, loving them, seducing them into singing beautiful harmonies. Every young player's waking thought goes toward learning new techniques to make their instrument sing. They sing out their passions, their joys, and laughter. They sing out their sadness and misgivings, their loves and desires toward the things, and the ones they love with equal passion, well into adulthood and professional years.

Often instruments are left as legacies passed on to future generations. They are not just bottom-line commodities whose worth is measured in dollars and cents. What price has music? It's true, professional players reap material rewards. But the real rewards are kept in the souls of those who love them and teach them to sing. And sing they did. You've seen them around the necks of the biggest stars in music and most likely heard them on records, in concerts, and on TV.

In life, they sang for the joy of all who dared master them. And they sang proudly for the lasting pleasure of all that heard them sing.

Ed Beaver, a guitar repairman in Nashville, summed it up: "This is the music version of the Louvre flooding."

Nashvillians, like most Americans, are resilient. One way or another, they bounce back from disasters. And when disaster

238

strikes, the most unlikely people band together with acts of kindness, generosity, and heroism. Generosity and heroism lived in abundance in Nashville after the flood. Every day, people helped their neighbors and got involved in rescue operations of flood-impacted neighbors and strangers alike. The music community responded with benefit concerts for those of lesser means. The days after the flood were proud days for American, Nashvillian, and "country" values.

In some ways, I regretted giving up Soundcheck, in other ways, not so much. Mainly I was glad the flood had not happened on our watch, though Toni and I would have handled it in our own way. We would have played it a little more on top of the beat, not behind it. We would have been a little more proactive in a rescue plan in the early stages. We still fantasize about it. After all, it had been our baby. We conceived it and built it and went through the growing pains as it grew and matured and became part of a larger family.

They say hindsight is 20/20, and I'm sure the new owners did the best they knew-how in handling the situation.

Other times I missed being of service to the music and the people who make it as I had done since my first road tours with Dan Fogelberg and his band in the late 1960s. They were, after all, the guys that gave me my name, the name that made me as famous among my peers as they were among theirs.

I did not miss the endless requests at Soundcheck for Eagle's stories. Once you've lived in and made it through legendary days, you can only relive them so many times. I'd long since moved on from those days. I wanted to live in the present. It wasn't about how I helped other people in their accomplishments anymore. It was at long last about my own.

Toni and I were proud of the business and the life we had built in Nashville, and we wanted to enjoy the benefits before the sun set over the hill for the last time.

Soundcheck Exterior and Main Entrance

Interior Construction

Myself, Joe's Friend, Joe Wlsh, My wife Toni

Joe Walsh onstage at Soundcheck's Grand Opening

completed Rehearsal Studio

Massive Flood Damage
At Sound Check Studios

FLOOD OF 2010

THE TENNESSEAN | SUNDAY, MAY 9, 2010 | A21

Volunteers turn out in force to aid victims

By Christine E. Sanchez

Corps struggled with dams, forecasts

CUMBERLAND RISING

Over the weekend of May 1-2, 2010 world renowned studio and vintage equipment storage center, Soundcheck Studios, in Nashville, TN suffered massive flood damage. Anybody that is somebody in the music business had equipment – guitars, amps, pianos, drums, etc. stored there.

Snakes that came up with the river were a real danger

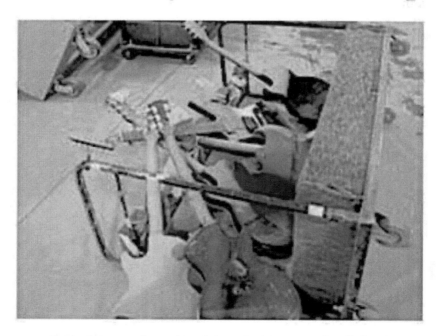

Overturned cart of flood damaged guitars

Guitar Graveyard

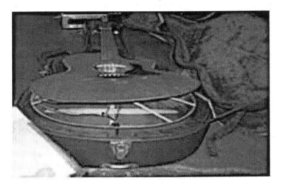

Flood Damaged Guitars

Water Level - Opry Backstage Door

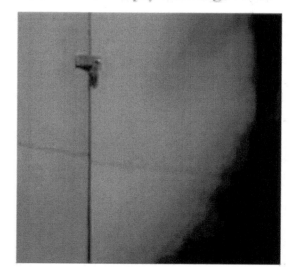

Water Level -Soundcheck Locker

25

Last Encore

It had been five years since the great Nashville flood, and everything had returned to the status quo. I'd long since sold Soundcheck and moved on. Glenn Frey, my business partner with an equal share in the business, had been paid in full from the sale's proceeds and then some. We'd both moved on with our lives.

Glenn was now a family man. He and Cindy were raising 3 kids. Toni and I were retired, living in Goodlettsville, Tennessee, and enjoying the quality of life, living on the proceeds from our end of the business. I had lost contact with Glenn, though I thought of him often. He played a significant role in my life for many years. He was my friend, my livelihood, and ultimately responsible for my eventual success as a business owner. I'd never forgotten that, and I never will. In all the roles Glenn played in my life, he had always been fun, fair, generous, and loyal, though he did have his moments, and I guess, so did I.

Overall, it had been a great ride.

By 2015 Glenn and I had faded far into the background of each other's lives. We lived on different planets in opposite solar systems, and we were both content with our lives as they were.

Sometime in 2015, I'm not sure exactly when I began hearing rumblings about Glenn having reoccurring bouts with illness. As far back as the 1980s, he had been forced to cancel gigs to deal with chronic intestinal problems. His rheumatoid arthritis had grown worse over the years.

Through the old Eagles "grapevine," I heard that Glenn had ulcerative colitis, and doctors wanted to remove all or part of his intestine. We heard that Glenn had been hospitalized in New York and placed in a medically induced coma as part of his colitis treatment.

In November of 2015, we were still just hearing rumors. No one knew for sure what was going on. We heard that Irving had gathered some of the top doctors in New York to give a prognosis. In November 2015, someone told us there was no hope for him, and the doctor's consensus was that he be taken off life support.

The next thing we heard, via rumor again, was that the family opted to not remove Glenn from life support in November to not ruin everyone's holidays and that a date in January had been chosen. The only information we were getting was hear-say at best and not coming from anyone in authority.

We were sort of out of the loop at that time. We weren't high enough in the food chain to get information directly, and the press certainly didn't know anything. There were a few undisputed authorities in the Eagles chain of command, and none of them were speaking publicly. We were grief-stricken and under a veil of sorrow over the fate of our beloved friend and my former employer. We were concerned but simply didn't know what was actually going on.

Then Glenn's old friend and mentor Bob Seger put an end to all the rumors. He laid out the facts in a tearful interview with internet news outlet Page Six:

"They were trying like hell to keep him alive. His manager pulled every ace out of the hole. He had the eight best specialists working on Glenn, but pneumonia worsened, weakening his immune system and aggravating the pre-existing conditions. First, he caught one set of pneumonia, then he caught a very virulent set of pneumonia. He was in a coma, and he'd come out, but then he couldn't breathe. They'd put him back in a coma," Seger said. "...They had to throw up their hands."

Glenn's brother Alan Frey said, "He fought to keep his final hospital battle a secret from the world. He hated talking about his worsening condition, and no one imagined how bad it really was until the very end."

News articles reported that Don Henley and his wife Sharon sat with Glenn's wife, Cindy, at Glenn's bedside near the end. On the third Monday of January, January 18, 2016, Glenn passed on. Then the whole world was officially notified.

Toni was friends on social media with one of my old Eagles crewmates. Word was that a big memorial service for Glenn would be held in LA, and those invitations were sent out. We never got one.

It hurt deeply to know that key members of the Eagles staff and crew and other casual acquaintances and celebrities were invited. I had devoted a greater portion of my life to looking after Glenn, and I had taken the seed money he provided as my partner in Soundcheck and made a huge profit for us both. Beyond all that, we had been friends, close friends. Some event planners had confirmed that we were not high enough on the food chain to be worthy of the opportunity to show our respects to the man we both loved.

Toni mentioned to our mutual friend on social media that we had not gotten an invitation. He found it hard to believe and offered to look into it. Later his response was, "They thought Norton was dead." We weren't sure how to take that. Were they sarcastic as in "We haven't heard from you in so long that we thought you were dead," or, "we thought you had literally died." It felt like a lame excuse, but our friend assured us we would get an invitation, and eventually, we did.

Toni and I flew to LA on the day of the memorial and sat through the 4-hour long remembrance that was, for the most part, like watching paint dry. During that testimonial portion, people that weren't personally close to Glenn spoke on and on. None of Glenn's kids spoke.

Then Joe Walsh, for all his reputation as a bad boy, performed a song on the piano he had written just that morning, delivered from deep in his gut. He never made it through the entire piece. Joe broke down, fighting back the tears to the end. Once again, Joe had opened a portal to the universe, and real emotion came pouring out. Joe was being Joe, and Joe was the real deal.

Irving Azoff introduced Don Henley.

When Henley stepped up to deliver the actual eulogy. Every eye and ear in the place were riveted on him.

Scenes of my time with Glenn scrolled through my head. The "nice catch" that had initially endeared us to each other, and the reward he bestowed on me. The time I had inadvertently upstaged him in front of the pro ballplayers at the baseball camp and how he busted my chops about it in the rented camper, all the way back to LA. The endless loop of scenes scrolled on, and I savored every single one.

Henley:

"He was like a brother to me; we were family, and like most families, there was some dysfunction. But the bond we forged 45 years ago was never broken, even during the 14 years that the Eagles were dissolved. We were two young men who made the pilgrimage to Los Angeles with the same dream: to make our mark in the music industry — and with perseverance, deep love of music, our alliance with other great musicians and our manager, Irving Azoff, we built something that has lasted longer than anyone could have dreamed."

My eyes misted, and my emotions rose to the surface, then overflowed as more scenes from my years with Glenn filled the inner screen of my mind. I pictured him, saying, "…One more time, and you're off the ice."

Henley:
"I'm not sure I believe in fate, but I know that crossing paths with Glenn Lewis Frey in 1970 changed my life forever, and it eventually had an impact on the lives of millions of other people all over the planet. It will be very strange going forward in a world without him in it. But I will be grateful for every day that he was in my life."

I, too, had been impacted by Glenn. For me as well, it had been strange going-on without Glenn in my life; getting off the road, working, and growing the business for us both. Becoming a 'citizen' again, becoming Bobby 'Norton' Thompson, husband, father, successful business owner, respected in the community, a revered baseball coach. I owed the journey, the opportunities, and the life lessons I got on the way to one person alone: Glenn Frey.

Henley wrapped up his eulogy with:

"Rest in peace, my brother. You did what you set out to do, and then some."

Henley's words hit home, and I could barely contain myself. I Found a table for Toni and me, and we parked ourselves there. Suddenly people began gravitating to our table, well-known musicians, former Eagles and Glenn Fry crew, and tour staff members. Our table was an island of non-pretension in a sea of condescension. At one point, Toni got up and said she was leaving us to get reacquainted with some folks. I think her words were, "OK guys, I'm getting up for a while, enjoy yourselves." Later Toni said, "I couldn't believe it, I looked back, and all these famous people were sitting at our table."

Cindy Frey came up to me, and we shared a joke about the notorious tapes from the Ireland gig that I had saved after Glenn said to "just burn them." She hadn't been there more than a minute when the Supreme Being swooped in and, without acknowledging my presence put his arm around her. In a very Hollywood way, he said something like, "Sweet Cindy come along with me, I have some people I want you to meet." It was insulting as if he rescued her from an unpleasant situation like I had done for Glenn countless times over the years. As he whisked her off, her young son cried-out that he was hungry. I offered to take him to where food was being served and look after him while she and Irving worked the room. She seemed relieved at that.

Wherever a room full of Hollywood entertainment types of any kind gather for any occasion, the atmosphere is thick with a glittery sparkle and buzz. Yet an air of underlying pretension and condescension exists as low-lying ground fog, barely visible to the untrained eye and ear. Many show up just to be seen, work the room, network with their peers, and affirm their elevated and elite status. Status in Hollywood demands the elite be seen amidst their peers, regardless of the occasion. Funerals and Memorials are especially interesting in Hollywood. Even death is an opportunity to work the room, one-up old rivals, and gloat over one's longevity over the deceased.

There is a legendary story from old Hollywood about John Ford, the director of many classic films. At actor Ward Bond's funeral, he commented on his former star's death. Ford turned to actor Andy Devine and said, "Now *you're* the biggest asshole I know." That became the final encore John Ford allowed Ward Bond.

Bandmates Don Henley, in his heartfelt comments, and Joe Walsh with his open display of profound grief, had allowed Glenn Frey's final encore the love, and class, and dignity he so well deserved.

Glenn's passing and his memorial marked *my* last encore as well. My time in entertainment and touring was over. I had come up through the ranks to successfully build and run Soundcheck, my last endeavor with touring musicians, bands, and entertainers.

It had made me financially comfortable, and I was officially retired. For *my* finale and *my* last encore, I came full circle at Glenn's memorial to touch bases with many of a previous life's cast.

Glenn's death and Henley's eulogy had touched me deeply. It had opened up a door, and past memories came rushing in. I tended to our 30 acres on the mountainside in Tennessee. I had a lot of time on my hands to think and reflect on a lifetime of memories. Impressions of my life's experiences frequently appeared before me. I didn't want to lose those memories. They might not follow me to whatever comes next. I wanted them preserved in this time and place before who I am now, Bobby "Norton" Thompson, leaves this place and moves on to the great unknown.

This book is my life review. I hope I passed

Acknowledgments

The situations depicted in this book are from the memory of Bobby "Norton" Thompson. The authors along with Toni Thompson, made a best effort to fill in foggy remembrances caused by the onset of aging, dementia, and almost forty years distance from the subject matter and the glory days experiences. We found background facts in books and other publications and by searching newspaper articles.

Five sources proved to be the most comprehensive and consistent.

Toni Thompson
A two-time cancer survivor, for her enthusiasm, energy, and clarity in plugging many holes with accurate details.

"To The Limit, The untold story of the Eagles"
By Mark Eliot

"Heaven And Hell My life In The Eagles 1974-2000"
By Don Felder with Wendy Holden

"Eagles The Ultimate Guide"
A Rolling Stone Special Edition Featuring Don Henley on the making of every album
And The 40 Greatest Songs

Newspapers.com

All of these sources were a great help to us in writing this book.

Sebastian Jaymes - Biography

Sebastian Jaymes grew up on the "North Coast of America" on the Great Lakes, near Lake Erie. At a very early age, he decided he wanted to see the world and did so first as a boy by exploring his home region and nearby states. In the 1960s, at the age of nineteen, he was able to fully realize that goal first as a roadie, then tour manager for two hit rock n roll bands. In the later 1960s and early 1970s, Jaymes worked with an up and coming band on a wild ride through the 60s counterculture.

In the early 1970s, settling in California, he found himself in the mainstream of the Los Angeles entertainment industry, at first as a roadie, or a PA on network TV variety shows. He returned to tour manage various celebrity artists, traveling the world over and realizing his childhood dream to "see the world on someone else's dime."

For fifteen years, he hired out as a Freelance producer of large corporate events and shows of all kinds in many exotic locales worldwide. ("I wanted to continue traveling internationally, so in between producing assignments I took on freelance projects as a live show technical director for corporate, TV, and live shows all over the world.") As freelance opportunities all but dried up in the economic slowdown of 2008, he continued a long relationship with USO as an independently contracted team member on celebrity entertainment events at military bases and in combat zones around the world.

He has a passion for American Civil War history and Archaeology and has visited battlefields, ancient ruins, and museums worldwide on his own dime. Jaymes currently lives in the Southern California desert and writes books and screenplays.

***

Sebastian Jaymes is the author of the memoir trilogy, "Memoirs From The Road To Everywhere."

Vol. I   The Road To Rock n Roll:
About growing up in Cleveland and finding a way to see the world on someone else's dime in Rock n Roll

Vol. II   Wild Boys and Girls Of The Road
Seeing the world with top artists Mac Davis, The Pointer Sisters, Neil Diamond, and others on Tour, in network television and in live music venues worldwide.

Vol. III Beyond The Far Horizon
The Authors worldwide adventures traveling in entertainment, personal travels, and as part of a team that put together celebrity entertainment events for the US military in war zones and at duty stations worldwide.

Look for a fiction book, an action-adventure thriller from this author featuring a female protagonist in late 2020 or early 2021.

Made in the USA
Columbia, SC
27 January 2021